*the casino handbook*

# THE CASINO
## HANDBOOK

BELINDA LEVEZ

BARNES
&NOBLE
BOOKS
NEW YORK

ISBN 0-7607-2735-X

Publisher: Mariëlle Renssen
Managing Editors: Claudia Dos Santos, Mari Roberts
Managing Art Editor: Peter Bosman
Editor: Gill Gordon
Designer: Sheryl Buckley
Illustrator: Anton Krugel
Picture researcher: Sonya Meyer
Production: Myrna Collins

Reproduction by Hirt & Carter (Pty) Ltd, Cape Town
Printed and bound in Malaysia by Times Offset (M) sdn Bhd

Although the author and publishers have made every effort to ensure that
the information contained in this book was correct at the time of going
to press, they accept no responsibility for any loss or inconvenience
sustained by any person using this book.

ABOVE *The interior of the pyramid at the Luxor, in Las Vegas.*

PREVIOUS PAGE *Slot machines, such as at Paris Las Vegas Casino, offer better odds than table games. The current trend is toward computer-enabled smart cards instead of coins.*

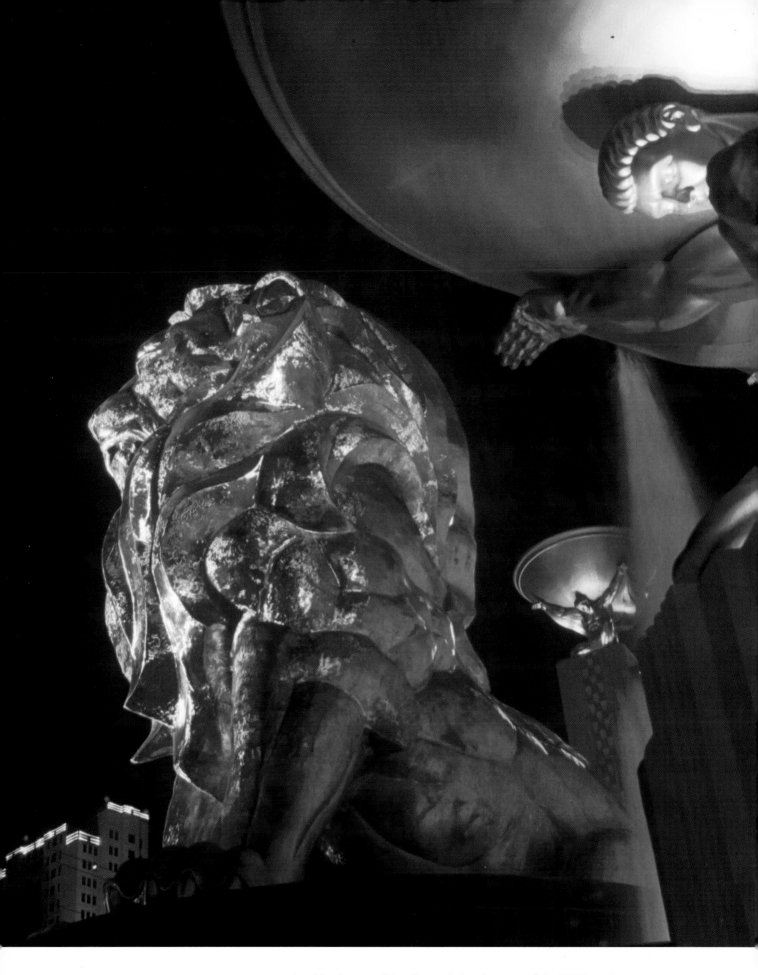

ABOVE *A golden lion, recalling the much-loved mascot of the MGM movie company, graces the entrance to the MGM Grand Casino in Las Vegas.*

# CONTENTS

# INTRODUCTION

Games of chance have been played for thousands of years and exist in virtually all cultures. Gaming is betting on the outcome of games, and despite many attempts throughout history to ban gaming, it has thrived. The games played in casinos today have evolved gradually over centuries and in different parts of the world.

Initially individuals would bet against each other. Later, gaming houses, or casinos, were established where people could bet against a banker with substantial funds. Since the mid-20th century, the widespread legalization of gambling and casinos has resulted in an enormous industry, generating huge profits and boosting the treasuries of many nations. In the U.S., over $26 billion per year is spent on gaming, and the state of Nevada raises more than 40 percent of its state tax revenue from Las Vegas casinos.

For players, an essential factor for success in gaming is understanding the aims and rules of play. Although most of the games are simple, the complex betting layouts and the terms used make them seem difficult to a beginner. Many casino visitors lack confidence. They learn by watching others and only play the easier games, such as roulette or the slots.

RIGHT *It's all in the fall of the cards. Whether you prefer cards, dice, or spinning wheels, there is a casino game for every player.*

Sometimes even experienced gamblers hesitate to try blackjack, craps, or baccarat, because they do not fully understand the rules. *The Casino Handbook* explains the basics of how to play the most popular games.

Gaming has its own unique language which can be unintelligible to the outsider, so throughout, "Game Speak" panels explain the terms used, helping the first-time visitor to enter into the spirit of the casino world.

Prominence has been given to Las Vegas which, after half a century in the business, remains the gaming capital of the world. The city attracts more than 33 million visitors annually, who spend $6 billion on 120,000 slot machines and 4000 gaming tables.

Nowadays, particularly in tourist-oriented destinations such as the Caribbean, South Africa, and Australia's Gold Coast, casinos are frequently incorporated into multifaceted resort-style vacation complexes, some of which are featured in this book. Gaming has come to be viewed as just another part of the worldwide tourism, leisure, and entertainment industry.

Gaming can be a pleasurable pastime, but it is easy to get carried away and exceed your limits. Casino visitors should remember that they are there to have fun and enjoy the experience—making a profit is an added bonus.

Staking levels and admission costs given throughout are intended only as a guide and were correct when going to press.

LEFT *The sound of slot machines in action echoes through casinos everywhere, promising instant fortune to the lucky few.*

# THE HISTORY AND ORIGINS OF GAMING

**B**ETTING games have been played since the earliest times in virtually all cultures. In ancient Egypt, Greece, and Rome, people used various devices to bet on the outcome of random events. Although the Greeks had a profound understanding of mathematics, they had no concept of probability, and assumed that the outcome of games of chance was due to the will of the gods. It was not until many centuries later that French mathematicians Pierre de Fermat and Blaise Pascal explored the mathematics of gambling, leading to the formulation of Pascal's theory of probability in 1654.

The first recorded betting games were played with marked disks or bones (the forerunners of dice), and spinning wheels or shields. Playing cards only came later, after the invention of paper. These three types of devices provided the basis from which modern casino games have evolved.

RIGHT *A Greek amphora, dating from c530BC, shows Ajax and Achilles playing with dice, which were most probably fashioned from knucklebones.*

LEFT *An image from a 14th-century Italian illuminated manuscript depicts playing or wagering with dice. The cube-shaped design is now evident.*

## FROM BONES TO COINS

Dice games have existed in one form or another for over 2000 years and were originally played with dice fashioned from the knucklebones of sheep. The Romans were fervent gamblers, and gaming scenes are depicted in wall drawings at Pompeii.

Some cube-shaped dice, carved from bone, were used with markings on all six sides, much like modern versions, while other dice had marks on just four sides. A variety of games was played, some using two dice, others using three. As the Romans conquered Europe, their games traveled with them and changed under the influence of different cultures.

By the 18th and 19th centuries a dice game called Hazard had become popular in England, and was played by the aristocracy in private gambling houses. The lowest possible score was a pair of ones—known as crabs. When the game was introduced to France, the word crabs was misinterpreted as "craps," giving one of the most popular casino games its name.

European settlers took the game with them to America, where it was simplified and evolved into the game that is now played in casinos around the world.

Two-up is another modern game that has its origins in Roman times, when coin tossing was a popular street game. Players would bet on whether the coin would land on heads or ships (tails). In England this developed into pitch and toss, using two pennies. When Australia was settled, pitch and toss continued to be played by the new immigrants. The game was popular with Australian and New Zealand Army Corps (Anzac) soldiers during World War I, when it became known as two-up. In Australia it became traditional to play two-up on Anzac Day.

BELOW *An etching by Thomas Rowlandson (c1787), depicting an altercation at a Hazard table, seems to suggest that when money is at stake, gentlemen do not always resolve disputes in a civilized manner.*

# SPINNING WHEELS

Soldiers in ancient Greece invented a game using a shield, which was spun on the top of a spear. They marked sections on the shield and placed bets on where the shield would stop. The Romans played similar games, using spinning chariot wheels. These evolved into the popular fairground wheel of fortune, the forerunner of today's casino game of big wheel six.

The origins of roulette are not well documented. French mathematician Blaise Pascal is often credited with inventing the roulette wheel as a result of his experiments with perpetual motion machines. One theory is that it derived from an old English game called roll it. A game called even-odd, which is played on a spinning wheel, is another contender; however, it is most likely that roulette evolved over time from a combination of games.

In 1842, Frenchmen François and Louis Blanc devised roulette with a single zero. Gaming was illegal in France at that time, but the new version was soon introduced in Hamburg, Germany, where it replaced an earlier version of roulette with two zeros.

When gaming started in Monte Carlo, François and his son, Camille, introduced their version using one zero and a haphazard arrangement of numbers, which became extremely popular in European casinos where it is still played today.

In the early 1800s the two-zero version of roulette arrived in America. It flourished in the saloons of the Old West during the California gold rush and Nevada silver era, when fortunes would be won or lost on the spin of the wheel. In American roulette, the numbers on the wheel are arranged in a more random fashion than is the case in Europe.

The significance of the extra zero is that it gives the house (the casino) a larger advantage, equivalent to twice that on the single-zero European wheel. Modern American casinos play both versions of the game.

RIGHT *In this old postcard, dating from around 1910, Lady Lottery is shown blowing lucky numbers while balancing on a wheel of fortune. Her dress is that of the cancan dancers who entertained early gamblers.*

Keno, the casino version of lotto, originated in China nearly 2000 years ago when Cheung Heung devised a lottery as a way of raising funds for his province's army. This proved to be a huge success and even funded the building of the Great Wall of China.

Lotteries were brought to America in the 1800s by the thousands of Chinese immigrants who worked in the mines and on the railroads. With the establishment of Las Vegas, the game was quickly adapted for casino play. Originally known as Chinese lottery, casinos throughout the world now operate keno games.

## PAPER CARDS

Paper was invented in China, and it is likely that playing cards also originate from that ancient empire. Domino cards, which are the earliest recorded type of playing cards, represented the scores thrown by a pair of dice, much like today's domino tiles.

Modern playing cards have evolved from ancient Chinese money cards, which comprised four suits (coins, strings of coins, myriads of strings, and tens of myriads of strings), each of which depicted various quantities of money.

By the 1370s, playing cards had reached Europe in a form that is recognizable today, with a pack consisting of 52 cards with suits of swords, polo sticks, cups, and coins. Each suit contained the numbers one to ten, and three court, or picture, cards. Originally the court cards were nonfigurative, but under European influence they soon became kings, knights, and valets. Queens later replaced the knights, and in England the valet became known as a jack.

The earliest cards were painted by hand with figures copied from manuscripts, but as printing developed the designs were continually altered and redrawn. There were national variations in the suit symbols. Italy adopted coins, cups, swords, and batons; while hearts, leaves, bells, and acorns appeared on German cards. The symbols on modern playing cards (hearts, spades, diamonds, clubs) originate from France.

With the widespread availability of cards, people began to invent card games. New games were continually being devised, many of which were played for money. In Europe, games like baccara proved popular among members of the aristocracy, who gambled for huge stakes in luxurious surroundings.

LEFT *Early playing cards were illustrated by hand with fanciful designs copied from manuscripts, as shown in this 1819 Cartes à Rire de Thalie Jeu des Théâtres.*

TOP RIGHT *Chinese money cards are not merely an early form of currency. They also represent some of the earliest known objects from which the concept and design of modern playing cards evolved.*

Although baccara has its origins in medieval Italy, it soon spread to France, where it was called chemin de fer (meaning railway, due to the action of the card box or shoe passing around the table on "tracks"). Later a slightly different version, called punto banco, arrived in England. Chemin de fer soon spread from Europe into Latin America. It was introduced to Las Vegas in the 1950s as a result of the closing of Cuban casinos. In Las Vegas it became known as shimmy, but is now mostly referred to as baccarat. Today, most casinos around the world offer a version of the game.

Poker is derived from the Persian game of *as nas* and was probably based on the dice game *tali,* which was played by the Romans. *Tali* is based on the ranking of throws where, for example, three of a kind beats a pair. A variation, called poker dice, is still played as a pub game in continental Europe. Persian sailors taught French settlers in New Orleans how to play *as nas,* and they developed a version which combined elements of the French game *poque* and the German game *pochen,* and became known as poker. This version was soon being played everywhere in the U.S., from Mississippi riverboats to the saloons of the Old West.

Many variations of the game started to appear. In 1911 U.S. legislation prohibited stud poker, but ruled that draw poker was a game of skill and therefore was not illegal. This resulted in new draw games being invented. Nowadays casinos offer a wide choice of poker games including five-card stud, seven-card stud, Texas hold 'em, and Omaha.

Blackjack derives from the game twenty-one, the origins of which are not known. When it was first introduced to casinos in the U.S. the game was not very popular, so the casinos started to offer odds of ten to one if 21 was made with the first two cards dealt to a hand (comprising an ace plus either the jack of spades or the jack of clubs—the "black jacks" from which the name derives). These higher odds no longer apply for 21 made with a black jack, but while any card with a face value of ten, together with an ace, counts as a score of 21, blackjack has become the name by which the game is known.

Blackjack began to rise in popularity after research undertaken by a trio of Americans showed that the casino's advantage could be overcome. Roger Baldwin was the first to begin analyzing blackjack and in 1956 published *The Optimum Strategy in Blackjack*. In 1962 Edward Thorp further developed the strategy into the first card counting techniques, which were published in his book *Beat the Dealer*. Julian Braun added to the earlier research on basic strategy in his book *Playing Blackjack as a Business*.

Casinos retaliated by making blackjack more difficult, implementing measures which make it harder for card counters to gain an advantage. As a result, blackjack has become a battle between players, who use a variety of card counting methods, and casinos, which try to handicap players by using multiple card decks, frequent shuffling, and surveillance. Many casinos ban players whom they suspect of card counting, despite court rulings that the practice is not illegal.

## SPORTS BETTING

A feature of many modern casinos are the sports books (facilities where betting takes place on horse races and other sporting events). Frank Rosenthal, a U.S. horse-racing handicapper who realized that bookmaking could be a huge money-maker for casinos, opened the first race and sports book at the Stardust Casino in Las Vegas. Its success resulted in race and sports books being introduced to The Strip. The story of Rosenthal's life was portrayed in the movie *Casino*.

BELOW *Modern sports betting relies on satellite broadcasting, but there was no less enthusiasm in the days when traveling fighters provided the entertainment.*

# SLOT MACHINES

In 1899, Charles Fey of San Francisco devised the Liberty Bell, the forerunner of modern slot machines. The coin-operated, one-armed bandits, as they became known, had a basic design of three spinning wheels marked with symbols. In 1905, the Mills Novelty Company of Chicago stole a machine and copied the design and, soon afterward, other companies began producing similar products.

Chewing gum was incorporated into the earliest versions, so that they could be classified as vending machines. This gave rise to the fruit symbols on the reels, indicating the flavors of the gum and hence the name "fruit machine." The symbol of a bell on the reels derives from the original Liberty Bell machine.

Slot machines spread rapidly across the U.S. until the 1950s, when federal legislation restricted their use.

Slot machines were originally introduced as an amusement for the wives and girlfriends of high-rolling gamblers, but by the 1980s slot machines were as popular as table games, and by the 1990s the slots had surpassed table games in popularity.

Las Vegas has more than 165,000 slot machines of every imaginable type. Their success is due to their simplicity, as no skill is required to play them. New machines are continually being developed—the latest trend incorporating video and computer technology into dynamic interactive games.

ABOVE *The Little Duke slot machine features three spinning disks, not reels, as in other early models. When it first appeared in 1932, at the height of the U.S. Depression, it cost just one penny per play.*

LEFT *The "One-Star" Chief Bell Machine, produced by the Jennings company between 1935 and 1936, was an immediate hit with vending machine operators, as its Western theme appealed to customers.*

# ESTABLISHING AN INDUSTRY

Before the establishment of casinos, gambling games were conducted on the streets, in homes, or in private clubs. (The word "casino" comes from the Italian *casa,* which means house.) The amount that could be won was limited to the funds of the individual players. By the 17th century, however, gambling had become formalized, with special venues that offered players the opportunity to bet against the "house," which would act as banker, paying out all winnings and retaining losing bets. This gave players the advantage of potentially winning more money than they bet.

## EARLY CASINOS IN EUROPE

One of the oldest casinos in Europe, at Baden Baden in Germany, was opened in 1748 by Edouard Benazet, who employed Parisian craftsmen to design the stylish rooms. Despite several closures in its history, the Baden Baden casino still operates today.

The casino at Spa, a Belgian resort town noted for its mineral baths, was built by the Prince Bishop of the province of Liège in 1763.

In 1857, Prince Charles III of Monaco decided to introduce gambling to his Mediterranean principality to boost its finances. Under the auspices of art lover François Blanc and his son, Camille, no expense was spared on the *belle époque* building which was created by a number of architects, among them Charles Garnier, designer of the Paris Opera House.

In the early 20th century, Monte Carlo Casino quickly became a fashionable destination for the rich and famous of the day, including the director of the *Ballet Russe* in Paris, Sergei Diaghalev, Britain's King Edward VII, and the Italian tenor Enrico Caruso.

RIGHT *Christian Bokelman's painting of the Monte Carlo casino depicts the sumptuous interior that attracted the crème de la crème of European society in the latter half of the 19th century.*

## GAMING IN THE U.S.A.

Some of the first casinos in America were established during the early 1800s in New Orleans, along the Mississippi River. Although, at that time, there were no casinos on the riverboats themselves, informal gambling was a popular way for travelers to pass the journey. Professional gamblers, called sharps, would target wealthy passengers and relieve them of their money. Gambling moved westward with the expansion of the railroads and flourished during the time of the California gold rush and the Nevada silver era.

Las Vegas in Nevada owes its success to the mobster Benjamin "Bugsy" Siegel, who organized gaming and bookmaking operations for the Mob (the Mafia). Due to a crackdown on gambling in the eastern U.S.A., Siegel moved west in the 1940s. During the Great Depression, gambling had been legalized in Nevada to increase revenue for the state, but what existed in Las Vegas at that time were a few decidedly down-market casinos that were frequented by the locals.

Siegel planned to open a luxurious hotel where the rich and famous could gamble and, after a failed attempt to take over an existing casino, he decided to build his own. Once Siegel had managed to convince the Mob to invest in his idea, building started, but costs escalated from initial estimates of $1.2 million to over $6 million, because everyone, including Siegel, was stealing money from the project. It is rumored that the palm trees were sold to the casino several times over, and that Siegel's girlfriend, Virginia Hill, was accumulating money in a Swiss bank account.

The Mob soon discovered Siegel's skimming and ordered him to be killed, but decided to give him a reprieve until after the opening.

The Flamingo Hotel and Casino finally opened on December 26, 1946. A huge party was organized, with many of the film stars of the day in attendance. The hotel was not finished, so the guests had nowhere to sleep. They partied for two days and then went home.

The Flamingo was a flop, and Bugsy Siegel was eventually killed by the Mob in 1947, but his dream of making Las Vegas into a gambling center survived.

TOP *Early Las Vegas was little more than a few tawdry buildings on either side of a patch of road. But that road has grown up to become The Strip, and the former desert oasis now blooms with neon lights.*

As other businessmen realized that Las Vegas had potential as a resort, investment flowed into the town. The Desert Inn Casino opened in 1950, followed by the Sands Casino in 1952, with the Dunes, and the Riviera opening in 1955.

Despite gambling being illegal, casinos continued to operate elsewhere in the U.S.A. thanks to widespread corruption in the police and government. One of the most luxurious "illegal" casinos was Chicago's Big House, which operated between 1929 and 1950. Run by associates of gangster Al Capone, it was elegantly furnished, with mahogany gaming tables, oriental rugs, and a free taxi service to shuttle players to and from Chicago's southside. The club was also the headquarters of a countrywide bookmaking operation.

### FROM MOB TO STATE CONTROL

During the 1950s virtually all the casinos in Las Vegas were controlled by the Mob. A U.S. Senate investigation into criminal activity in the casino industry found that skimming (retaining a portion of the profits) was rife, resulting in tax evasion on stakes and profits.

When legislation allowing corporations to own Las Vegas casinos came into being in 1965, entrepreneur and multimillionaire Howard Hughes was the first to take advantage of this change in the law, buying the Desert Inn and several other casinos, as well as plots of land in the city. When MGM, Hilton, and Holiday Inn followed suit, the finances of the Mob proved to be no match for the might of the major corporations, and gradually the casino industry was cleaned up.

## OPPOSITION TO GAMBLING

In many countries, gambling has gone in and out of favor depending on the prevailing moral, social, and religious climate. Most objections to gambling are based on social and religious issues. However, despite numerous attempts throughout history to outlaw gaming, it has still thrived. Banning gaming simply results in the establishment of illegal casinos.

Gaming-related social problems are as old as gambling itself. In Roman times, gaming was restricted to one week of the year, during the Saturnalia festival (equivalent to the Christmas and New Year holidays). However, this did not deter Roman players, who continued to gamble in private houses and clubs. Even when fines (equivalent to four times the stakes) were introduced for players caught gambling, the Romans managed to evade the law by using engraved disks, called roundels, instead of money.

Almost as soon as playing cards were introduced to Europe, they were opposed. In Paris, legislation prohibiting playing cards was passed in 1377, and in Italy, playing cards and dice were burned.

In the U.S.A., many attempts were made to prevent gambling. Early Puritan settlers initially banned the possession of gaming equipment, but relented, allowing games for recreational purposes. Later legislation was ineffective, as it banned specific games. Players simply changed the names or invented new games. By 1910, gambling was made illegal throughout the U.S.A., but due to widespread corruption among law enforcement officers, this law had little effect.

RIGHT *Legendary entertainer Frank Sinatra, seen here onstage in the Copa Room at the Sands Hotel, was a regular on the Las Vegas circuit in the early days. His alleged Mob connections only added to his intrigue.*

# THE GAMING INDUSTRY TODAY

Studies have shown that today's casino players are typically graduates in white-collar jobs with a higher than average income, who gamble to win money. A survey carried out by Roper Starch Worldwide Inc. of New York found that, for three out of four casino visitors, their prime motive is to win, while 57 percent go for entertainment and recreation. Australians are the western world's biggest gamblers, spending over $2000 a year per head of population. A close second are Americans, at $1800 per head of population.

Casinos operate around the world, mainly in tourist areas including Las Vegas, Australia's Gold Coast, and resorts in the Mediterranean and Caribbean. Gaming is mostly controlled by the state, and is an important contributor to national and local revenues, although percentages vary from country to country.

Gaming is a huge industry in the U.S.A., where it is legal in 24 states. There has been a casino building boom in recent years, particularly in Nevada. Gambling was legalized in Atlantic City, New Jersey, in 1978, to revitalize the rundown resort.

In 1987, after a legal battle, the U.S. Supreme Court finally recognized the right of Native Americans to operate gaming establishments on their reservations. Since 1989, over 300 new gaming operations have been established on Indian reservations. The largest casino in the world, Foxwoods Resort in Connecticut, is owned and operated by the Mashantucket Tribe and attracts over 16 million visitors annually. It comprises two hotels and five separate casinos. Foxwoods has 1.5 million sq ft (140,000m²) of floor space, of which 300,000 sq ft (28,000m²) is devoted to gaming.

Las Vegas reigns supreme as the "casino capital" of the world, attracting 30 million visitors annually to over 50 casinos. When Wilbur Clark opened the Desert Inn on April 24, 1950, he ceremonially threw away the keys, announcing there would never be a need to lock the door again. That tradition continues today, with most Las Vegas casinos open 24 hours a day, seven days a week. The minimum age for gambling in Nevada is 21 years.

ABOVE *At the Fremont Street Experience, in downtown Las Vegas, a four-block-long canopy, lit by more than two million light bulbs, has created a vibrant pedestrian mall featuring bars, restaurants, and casinos.*

The 1960s saw the legalization of gaming in the U.K. Bringing the gaming industry within the law led to the implementation of strict controls to regulate payouts and how the games operate. The Gaming Board of Great Britain ensures the fair running of casinos and scrutinizes casino personnel and operators. Of the U.K.'s 116 casinos, 21 are located in London, with the remainder in major cities and tourist areas.

Almost all countries in continental Europe have casinos. France has government-regulated casinos in over 170 towns and cities. Spain legalized casinos in the late 1970s and also allows slot machines in bars and arcades. In the Netherlands, a government company, Holland Casinos, was established to operate the casinos, which now exist in ten locations. Greece has nine casinos, which are privately-run, government-allocated franchises. Belgium's eight casinos remain illegal, but are tolerated by the government, which imposes taxation on them.

In the 1970s casinos were legalized in Australia. They are run by private operators under franchises granted by the government. Fourteen casinos now operate in the major cities and Gold Coast resorts, contributing A$2 billion annually to state revenues.

Canada began opening government-owned casinos in the early 1990s, and now has a number of resort casinos that attract tourists, as well as some smaller provincial casinos catering for the local population.

Although South Africa introduced casino gaming during the apartheid era, confining it to the so-called "independent homelands," the demise of apartheid meant that the country had to face up to the reality of legalizing gaming operations that were formerly not considered to be within the boundaries of the state. Casino gaming was recognized in 1994 and a rationalization process, under the Gambling Board, has ensured that lucrative gaming licenses are equitably distributed throughout all nine provinces.

RIGHT *The latest innovations in computer technology are a feature of on-line, or Internet, casinos which use easy access and vibrant graphics to attract unwary gamblers and quickly part them from their money.*

## VIRTUAL CASINOS

The expansion of the Internet has seen a huge proliferation of on-line casinos. The sites are very appealing, encouraging browsers to enter by offering a variety of incentives to attract players, such as free trials of the games and prize-winning competitions.

The biggest problem with these sites is the lack of regulation. Whereas land-based casinos are subject to strict legislation, no such controls exist for on-line gambling sites. There are no laws in place to ensure that players get a fair deal, and no legislation guaranteeing minimum payouts. Furthermore, no controls exist to prevent children from accessing the sites, and there have been many calls to ban them altogether.

Many Internet gambling sites are run as offshore companies, and it is often difficult to trace the owners. If a player gets into a dispute with one of these companies, it is highly unlikely that he or she will get their money back. The best advice is to completely avoid virtual casinos and to stick to gambling in traditional casinos that are properly controlled.

# THE
# CASINO

*Stepping into another realm*

# EXPERIENCE

A CASINO embodies the concept of a luxurious, glamorous, and timeless environment, which has its own language, currency, and etiquette. Casinos provide the location and facilities for players to try their luck at a wide range of gambling games, in which the casino acts as banker, paying out winning bets and collecting losing bets. Working under strict controls aimed at preventing cheating, professional dealers, often called croupiers, operate the games, which include roulette, blackjack, baccarat, poker, craps, and slot machines. In general, casinos can be divided into two categories. City-center casinos tend to be more formal, imposing stricter dress codes and relatively high minimum stakes. Resort and smaller provincial casinos, which are usually more relaxed, allow casual wear and offer lower minimum stakes.

RIGHT *The lure of instant riches draws visitors to Auckland's Sky City, but the reality is that really big wins are made by only a small proportion of gamblers.*

LEFT *The fantasy world of modern casinos owes much to the imagination of the architects and designers who conjure up elaborate themes to appeal to visitors.*

Casino operators spend vast sums of money on lavish decor to attract customers. The most flamboyant concepts and designs are found in Las Vegas and other popular vacation resorts around the world. European casinos, especially those in cities, are often less ornate.

Once inside the casino, the interiors are carefully designed to keep players there. Windows and clocks are absent, to make the passing of time less noticeable. Waiters bring refreshments directly to the gaming tables, so there is no need to stop gambling if you are hungry or thirsty. Many casinos also provide in-house entertainment such as variety shows or revues, to keep players and nonplayers amused.

Guests at casino hotels and day visitors to casinos are not necessarily afforded any special treatment, but high rollers (regular gamblers who are known to be big spenders), get V.I.P. treatment at their favored casinos. They are provided with extras such as free hotel accommodation, meals and drinks, the best seats for shows, and chauffeur-driven limousines. They may even be flown in on specially chartered jets.

## THE PHYSICAL ENVIRONMENT

Casinos are often busy, noisy places. In European casinos, the quieter games, such as roulette and blackjack, are the most popular; while in the U.S.A., slot machines and craps are favored. On roulette, frenzied betting is interspersed with calm as players watch the wheel to see the winning number. By contrast the craps tables are the noisiest in the casino, with players cheering and shouting and constant commentary from the stickman (see page 73). The card tables tend to be more sedate, with players concentrating on the hands they have been dealt.

Away from the hustle and bustle of the gaming halls, most casinos have private rooms (called *salons privés*) to cater for the high-staking players who prefer to bet in a secluded environment.

Resort casinos, and most U.S. casinos, are usually part of large leisure complexes that include hotels, restaurants, and a range of entertainment and sports facilities. The gaming floors are often huge, with row

upon row of slot machines, including linked machines promising huge jackpot payouts. They have separate rooms or areas for keno (which is played in a theater-like arena), and baccarat, which attracts big spenders. Most casinos in Europe tend to be small intimate club-style establishments, and are often located in or near the center of the city.

The first area encountered on a visit to a casino is the lobby or entrance hall. Here reception personnel provide information and assistance to visitors and deal with any membership formalities. At some casinos, car valets take care of parking, while at others, huge parking lots may be located some way from the complex, with visitors transported via shuttle-bus or monorail. Cloakrooms or lockers may be provided to take care of coats and valuables.

Electronic items like mobile phones, computers, calculators, and radios are not allowed on the gaming floor. Taking photographs is also not permitted.

To reach the gaming tables, players generally have to pass through the noisy, vibrant slot machine area. Slots are easy to play, and the stakes tend to be low, so the slot halls are usually crowded. Flashing lights, bells and sirens, and the clatter of coins being paid out all add to the excitement. All types of mechanical and electronic games, from the old-fashioned, one-armed bandits to video poker, can be played, and interactive video games are becoming increasingly available.

The main gaming halls are lavishly decorated, often to a theme, but the focal points are the green or blue baize-covered tables, which are printed with betting layouts. Seating for players is provided around the tables, which are arranged in groups, called pits.

LEFT *An intricate sculpture, called* Fiori di Como, *by artist Dale Chiluly, graces the foyer of The Bellagio Hotel in Las Vegas. It comprises over 2000 flowers, each one handcrafted from colored glass.*

TOP RIGHT *A new way to "break the bank"? Casinos make it increasingly easy for players to get more money with less effort—even going so far as to put cash machines right on the gaming floor.*

A dealer or croupier runs the game at each table, and groups of tables are watched over by inspectors. Pens and paper are supplied for players to note the numbers spun on roulette, although nowadays, electronic signs at each roulette table indicate the last numbers spun.

Casinos in the U.S.A. often incorporate bookmakers. Called the race and sports book, the "bookies" take bets on horse racing, greyhound racing, and sporting events from around the world. Satellite broadcasts of major events are shown on huge screens, allowing players to watch in a theater-like environment.

At the cash point or the cage, in the main gaming area, a variety of financial transactions are carried out, such as cashing checks, applying for credit, exchanging money for chips, and cashing in winnings. Players can use local or foreign currency, or traveler's checks to purchase chips. Some casinos accept foreign currencies at the gaming tables, but most require money to be exchanged beforehand at the cash point.

Credit cards are not always readily accepted, and the amounts that can be cashed on them are limited. Where casinos allow credit betting, applications can be made at the cash point, or in advance by phone, mail or e-mail. Most casinos now have automatic teller machines (A.T.M.s) located near the cash point.

## PRIVATE ROOMS

Private rooms, called *salons privés* in Europe, are found mostly in the higher staking casinos, and are reserved for medium to high-staking players, allowing them to bet in a more secluded environment away from spectators. Private rooms, which are staffed by the casino's most experienced dealers, contain tables for games like roulette, blackjack, and baccarat. Favored customers, the really high rollers, are often afforded the privacy of a totally private room for their exclusive use.

## MEMBERSHIP REQUIREMENTS

In some countries, casinos require players to become members before they will admit them. Applications for membership must be made either in person or in writing, depending on the casino's rules. The straightforward procedure requires prospective members to give personal details such as name and address, and a dec-

laration that they are old enough to gamble.

The minimum age for gambling is usually the age of majority, commonly 18 years. In the U.S.A., players must be over 21, and in Switzerland over 20. Identification, such as a passport or driver's licensce, may be requested.

Membership is a legal requirement for entry into most British casinos. Players must apply 24 hours beforehand and must provide identification. Casinos reserve the right to refuse membership applications. A player who is barred from one casino may find it difficult to obtain membership for another, as the names of barred members are often circulated to other casinos within a group or in the same area.

TOP *The* salon privé, *or private room, is for high rollers, gamblers who are willing to play for higher minimum stakes than those in the main gaming hall.*

## DRESS CODE

Casinos reserve the right to refuse entrance to players who do not meet required dress codes. Casinos may have different standards for daytime and evening gaming, with more relaxed rules during the day. Up-market casinos, especially those that require membership, often insist that players are smartly dressed, with men expected to wear a jacket and tie. Resort casinos generally allow casual wear at all times, but the rules for individual establishments can vary considerably, so it is best to check the requirements before setting out. Jeans, T-shirts, beach wear, sports attire, and manual work clothes are often not allowed.

## CASINO PERSONNEL

All casino personnel wear uniforms, to easily identify their position. These are often a variation on evening wear, with the men wearing bow ties and waistcoats, and the women in long dresses. Inspectors, pit bosses, and managers are traditionally dressed in formal suits or tuxedos. General managers usually wear business or dress suits. In resort casinos, which often have a strong decor theme, uniforms tend to be less formal and frequently reflect the overall design concept.

Each table is operated by at least one dealer, who is responsible for running the game and operating the equipment. On card tables (blackjack and poker), this includes shuffling and dealing the cards. On roulette, the dealer spins the ball. The dealer's duties vary with each game, but generally include changing money into chips, placing player's bets, giving instructions about the game, paying out winning bets, and collecting losing bets on the casino's behalf, and monitoring players' behavior.

Inspectors watch over the tables. They are responsible for checking that the dealer is operating the game correctly, and that players are neither cheating nor being cheated. Each inspector may monitor more than one table. He or she checks large payouts and keeps records of how much each player spends and wins. The inspector notes how many high denomination chips are given to a player, and resolves any disputes that may arise between dealers and players.

If a problem occurs, such as a player not agreeing with the amount the dealer has paid out for a winning bet, or a winning chip being cleared away in error, the dealer will summon the inspector by making a kissing noise. This sound is used as it is easily heard through the noise of a casino. As all table games are recorded on videotape, any disputes are easily resolved.

Each group of tables is controlled by a pit boss, who is responsible for allocating staff to the tables and for checking the work of the dealers and the inspectors. The pit boss collates information about how much an individual player is spending and passes this on to the managers. He or she also collates details about how much a specific player is winning. This information is then relayed to the cash point, so when the player cashes in at the end of a gaming session, the cashier knows that the chips have been legitimately won, and were not acquired by cheating or pickpocketing.

BELOW *Dealers are always friendly and well-groomed and their uniforms are both practical and stylish.*

Casino managers deal with the day-to-day running of the casino. They socialize with players and allocate complimentary benefits (comps) such as drinks, meal vouchers, cigarettes, hotel rooms, or show tickets.

A player's level of spending determines what comps he or she receives, with the highest staking customers sometimes receiving everything free. Regular slot machine players can join a special club, which allows them to accumulate points that count towards comps.

Casinos may keep records of how much individual players win or lose. In countries where casinos are state controlled, these records may be scrutinized by government agencies, such as tax offices. As a control against money laundering (see Game Speak), governments may require casinos to supply details of players who regularly spend large amounts of money. Casinos in the U.S.A. are obliged to notify the Internal Revenue Service (I.R.S.) of U.S. citizens with big winnings.

Security staff constantly mingle with players. Some are uniformed, while others wear plainclothes. Casinos use a variety of electronic surveillance systems, sometimes called the "eye in the sky," to monitor the action on the gaming floors. All games are recorded, and the tapes are stored for a period of time, so that in the event of a dispute they can be played back.

While uniformed security personnel keep a lookout for pickpockets and chip snatchers on the gaming floors, behind-the-scenes staff watch the surveillance cameras. If a player is suspected of cheating, he or she will be closely watched from the control room. Players caught cheating will be photographed before being thrown out. Casinos share information about cheats, and their details are quickly circulated. Being caught cheating can result in a player being refused entry to all other casinos in the vicinity.

BELOW *In the security control room, trained personnel constantly monitor the action at the tables and on the gaming floor, looking for any evidence of cheating.*

## CASINO CURRENCY

Instead of playing with money, gamblers use colored plastic or metal disks, called chips. This enables the games to run quickly and smoothly, as the chips can be piled up into stacks and easily counted. Players can purchase chips at the cash point (in any currency), or on the gaming tables (in the local currency).

Each casino has its own exclusive set of chips that can only be used in that particular establishment. If a casino is part of a group, it may be possible for cash chips from one location to be used at another casino in the group, but it is best to confirm this before removing any chips from a casino.

There are two types of chips—cash chips and table chips. Cash chips are the casino's general currency. They can be used to buy into any games, place bets,

TOP *A variety of high denomination chips and plaques from Sun City Casino in South Africa. Each casino's chips are unique and cannot be used anywhere else.*

RIGHT *When cash (or cash chips) are exchanged for table chips, the stack is broken down by the dealer to prove that the correct amount is being handed over.*

pay for food and drinks and to tip the staff. Each chip is marked with the cash value, the name of the casino, and the casino's logo. Cash chips are often referred to by their color. For example, in London casinos £5 chips are called reds, £25 chips are blacks, £100 chips are pinks, and £1 chips are referred to as singles.

Lower denomination chips are disk-shaped (round). Higher denomination chips, called plaques or biscuits, are rectangular or oval. On leaving the casino, all cash chips are normally returned to the cash point to be exchanged for money or a check.

Table chips are only used for playing the game on a particular table. Chips from different tables can be distinguished by the colors and designs printed on them. They are not valid at other tables, but may be used for tipping staff. To buy table chips, you simply place your money or cash chips on the table, making sure they are not on the betting layout, and ask the dealer for "color." The dealer will give you table chips to the corresponding value. For ease of handling and counting, table chips are kept in stacks of 20. To prove that the correct number of chips is being handed over, the dealer will cut a stack into four piles of five chips, and spread out one of the piles to show five single chips. Before leaving a gaming table, ask the dealer to exchange your table chips for cash chips.

Some casinos allow players to bet by placing cash directly onto the betting layout. The dealer exchanges it for a special marker, announcing "money plays." If a cash bet wins it will be paid out in chips.

# CASINO ETIQUETTE

Players are expected to abide by a number of conventions in order to facilitate the smooth running of the games. These can be summed up as follows:

• Do not engage the dealer in conversation
• Do not put money or chips into the dealer's hand
• Do not throw chips or money at the betting layout
• Never move another player's bet
• Give up seats to players if you are watching.

Although all dealers are trained to be friendly and welcoming, they must also pay attention to the game and be alert for cheats. If you try to engage a dealer in casual conversation he or she may ignore you, as distracting dealers is a trick frequently used by cheats. If you need assistance, the best person to approach is one of the floor managers, as their duties include socializing with players. If you have a query about a game, ask the dealer to call an inspector.

ABOVE *Spills can disrupt games, so drinks should not be placed directly on the tables. Cash chips can be used to pay for drinks and other refreshments.*

Security requirements prevent dealers from taking anything directly from a player's hand, or possessions such as purses or jacket pockets. Dealers are also not allowed to shake hands with players, to prevent them from covertly passing across chips.

Throwing chips at the betting layout can result in other bets being knocked away from the correct place. On large tables, such as roulette and baccarat, if you cannot reach the area where you want to place a bet, simply put the chip on the table in front of you and call out loudly and clearly to the dealer where it should go. The dealer will repeat your instructions and place the bet. Unless you are actually buying chips or betting, never put money, cash chips, or table chips directly onto the table or the betting layout, as it will be assumed that you are making a bet.

On roulette, the first player to bet with cash chips takes precedence, and no one else may bet with the same value cash chips. Other players will be warned that someone is betting with cash chips, as the dealer will announce, for example, "reds on" or "pinks on" (depending on the color of the cash chips).

Do not leave your chips unattended at the tables, as it is quite likely that they will be stolen. The exception is poker, where the dealer will watch a player's chips during a leave of absence from the table.

Never straighten up or move another player's bet. If you need to place your chips on top of someone else's chips and their bet is ambiguously placed, query the bet with the dealer before making any moves.

Players should not touch any gaming equipment or cards unless instructed to do so by the dealer. In some casinos, blackjack players are not allowed to touch the cards at all, while in poker, where players hold their own cards, the cards must be kept in view at all times.

Players should wait until all the winning bets have been paid out before placing bets on the next game. The dealer will give the cue by announcing "place your bets" when it is time for the next game to begin.

Dealers have set procedures that they must follow, such as paying out all winning bets in a specific order—so even though you may be in a hurry to leave the casino, it is useless to request that your bet is paid out before your turn.

# GAMES PLAYED

Most casinos offer a wide choice of games, loosely based on the three basic items of equipment used in gaming—cards, dice, and wheels. Mechanical games (those that use wheels or other moving equipment) include roulette, slots, boule, big six wheel, and a form of lottery called keno. Craps, two-up, and sic-bo are all played with dice, or tokens such as coins. Card games include blackjack, poker, baccarat (also called chemin de fer or punto banco), and red-dog.

The games played in casinos vary from country to country. Some games have a number of international variations which are known by different names, while others are seldom played outside their country of origin. Poker, craps, and slot machines are commonly found in the U.S.A. and in international resort casinos, whereas European casinos tend to have traditional games, like French roulette, boule, and chemin de fer. Two-up is confined to Australian casinos. As the name suggests, Caribbean stud poker is particularly popular in that region, although it is also played elsewhere.

Casino cards are usually larger than normal playing cards. The two standard packs or decks of cards used widely in casinos, English-language cards and French-language cards, differ only in the symbols marked on the court or picture cards. In the English pack the King, Queen, and Jack are marked with the symbols K, Q, and J respectively, while the French cards use R, D, and V (standing for *Roi, Dame,* and *Valet*). Although the symbols differ, the cards are easily identified by the pictures, and players using an unfamiliar deck should not be confused. (In this book, English cards have been used throughout to illustrate the games.)

Many casinos produce leaflets outlining the various rules and providing brief details on how to play each of the games. Some casinos also give lessons at quieter times of the day, enabling players to try the games and learn the rules without losing any money.

ABOVE *French playing cards use different terms for the court cards, although the pictures are similar to the English-language cards used in most casinos.*

TOP *Slot machines were originally based on the simple mechanics of spinning wheels, but electronic and video slots are fast replacing traditional machines.*

## STAKES

Casinos impose both minimum and maximum stakes on each table game. The minimum stake is the lowest amount that can be bet on a game; the maximum is the highest amount that may be bet. However, within each game, the stake levels on different tables may vary. For example, in roulette, some tables will offer a low minimum stake (for example $5), while others have a higher minimum stake (such as $10). To enter a game, players **must** bet the minimum amount. Though they have the **option** of betting up to the maximum stake, it is not mandatory.

A sign on the gaming table, or suspended above it, indicates the table stakes. Each game has different stakes, and individual bets may differ within the stake level. The value of the table chips is automatically the value of the minimum stake. The lowest staking tables are often the most crowded, and the highest staking tables are generally located in the *salon privé*.

Bets within a game may also vary. On roulette, for example, the minimum stake on the outside bets may be higher than the minimum on the inside bets (see page 44). Although the value of the color (table) chips is automatically the minimum stake, customers may request a higher value. For example, the minimum stake on a roulette table may be $2 (meaning that each color chip is worth $2). If a player requests that his or her chips are marked to, say $25, a special marker is used to denote the new value of the chips.

Casinos often have lower minimum stakes during the quieter midweek period, increasing the stakes over weekends and vacations, when the casino is busy.

## FAIRNESS OF THE GAME

Strict controls are in place to ensure that players get a fair deal. Gaming is state controlled in most countries, where a combination of government legislation and gaming control agencies ensure that casinos pay out a reasonable return to players, and that all the gaming equipment used is fair and accurate.

Modern gaming equipment is state-of-the-art and precision-made. Items are checked regularly to ensure that nothing has been tampered with to give players or the casino an unfair advantage. Roulette wheels are frequently serviced, and their balance is checked.

The shoes or boxes for dealing cards are chained to the table to stop players switching them for cold decks (see Game Speak on pg 155). Before play, the cards are spread out to show that full decks are being used, and creased or marked cards are replaced. Any cards that become marked during play are immediately replaced.

TOP *Fresh cards are loaded into shoes before the start of each day's play. Card shoes are regularly checked to ensure that they have not been tampered with.*

LEFT *This sign on a blackjack table lets players know that it is a high-staking game. Beginners would be well advised to try a table with a low minimum limit.*

At the end of a day's gaming, the old cards are counted to ensure that none has been removed. They are then discarded. Before starting each new game, the cards are thoroughly shuffled, first by mixing them face down, and then by riffle shuffle (see Game Speak on page 155). A player is always invited to cut the cards by inserting a blank card into the pack.

Gaming dice are precision-made perfect cubes. They are transparent, to make it impossible to load them (see Game Speak on page 155). During play, the dealers continually scrutinize the dice to check they have not been switched for ones with a different arrangement of dots, or have filed edges or rounded corners, as these may make it easier to throw winning numbers. New dice are used each day and destroyed at the end of play, either by being marked with a special stamp, or by having a hole drilled through them.

The action on the gaming floors and at the tables is recorded on videotape and stored. Back-office security staff not only watch the players, but also the dealers, to ensure that they are not cheating by colluding with players. If there is any discrepancy, or if a player has a query over an aspect of a specific game, management can request that the relevant tapes be viewed.

Casino personnel are usually subjected to scrupulous checks before being employed. In the U.K., for instance, dealers are required to be individually licensed. Before a license is granted, prospective staff are carefully assessed, and their backgrounds are thoroughly checked. The police or gaming board officials may even visit their homes. In the U.K., dealers are not allowed to visit other British casinos in their free time. If found on the premises of another casino, their licenses are immediately revoked.

In most countries, companies that operate casinos are also subjected to stringent licensing procedures, often requiring months of careful investigation by gaming board officials. The lure of lucrative gaming licenses frequently leads to elaborate bidding contests between competitors keen to cash in on what has become accepted as a viable and profitable part of the global leisure and entertainment industry.

Most governments have realized that substantial revenues can be had from gaming, and they levy large annual operating fees—which casinos regard as just one more part of the cost of doing business in an industry that has grown from Mob control to megadollar conglomerates in only a few decades.

ABOVE *Before the day's play begins, decks of cards are thoroughly mixed before being shuffled, to ensure they are used in a truly random order.*

ABOVE *Shuffling machines now perform one of the dealer's tasks. They are fast, efficient, accurate, and more importantly, are not subject to human error.*

# ROULETTE AND SLOTS

*Games of chance where the chances are high*

GAMES of chance involve mechanical equipment, and therefore have an element that the player cannot control. Slot machines and roulette are the most popular and widely played casino games, as they appeal both to novices and more experienced players.

Casinos in Europe have a long tradition of playing roulette, but the game is less popular in the U.S.A., where the casino has a bigger house advantage due to the addition of an extra zero. Apart from this amendment, roulette has remained virtually unchanged for hundreds of years.

Slots account for more than 60 percent of gaming revenues in American casinos. This is because slots are easy to play and offer potentially huge returns for a relatively small stake. New technology constantly produces more sophisticated games.

RIGHT *A moment of suspense before the ball drops. The roulette wheel is one of the most dominant motifs of the casino world.*

LEFT *Roulette is a game of chance which requires little skill on the part of the player.*

ABOVE *The betting layout printed on the roulette table enables players to place a variety of bets, increasing their chances of winning. This version of American roulette, using only one zero, is popular in the U.K. and Europe.*

# AMERICAN ROULETTE

American roulette, which is played with two zeros, is derived from the original French version, played with only one zero (see page 50). Casinos particularly like the American version, because it is cheaper to run than French roulette and only needs one dealer to operate the game. American roulette is also more profitable, as the bets come flooding in at a faster rate.

American roulette is played on a large table which is printed with a betting layout. At one end of the table, a wheel encased in a wooden cylinder turns on a central spindle. The wheel is divided into 38 sections, numbered from zero to 36 inclusive, plus a section numbered double zero (00).

Consecutive numbers are arranged opposite each other on the wheel. Each number is colored either red or black, and the zeros are colored green.

The aim of roulette is to predict the number on which a ball spun around the wooden cylinder will land. The ball is spun by hand by a dealer and must make at least three revolutions before dropping into one of the numbered sections on the wheel. The ball moves in the opposite direction to which the wheel is spun. Each new spin starts from the previous number.

Predicting the winning number is made more difficult by the dealer, who can spin the ball at differing speeds by applying more or less pressure to the ball. The rate at which the wheel spins is also constantly changed. Before spinning the ball, the dealer may speed up or slow down the wheel. Diamond-shaped bars arranged around the lower part of the wooden casing help deflect the ball as it drops into the wheel. Dealers are also changed at regular intervals, as individual dealers each have their own pace and rhythm.

Roulette chips can only be used on the table to which they correspond. Their value is automatically

the minimum bet on that table. If players want the chips to have a higher value they simply inform the dealer, who will position markers to denote the chips' new value, which may be up to the table maximum.

Although roulette players may bet with cash chips, it is advisable to play with table chips (also called "color") to avoid disputes. If a player does start betting with cash chips, the dealer will call out "reds on" or "blacks on," for example, depending on the value of the chips. This warns other players not to bet with the same color cash chips.

The dealer controls the running of the game by giving a number of verbal instructions which indicate each stage of the game. To ensure that their bets are correctly placed, players should listen to the dealer. If a player accidentally knocks another player's chip out of position, the dealer will straighten up the bet and announce that a chip has been moved by calling out the color and the position where it has been placed. One player may not touch another player's chips.

Every casino has its loyal band of system hunters—players who sit for hours at the roulette tables, noting the winning numbers spun and analyzing the results in the hope of finding a winning formula. Casinos even supply paper and pencils for this purpose, confident in the knowledge that all the variables make this task virtually impossible.

RIGHT *Each player uses differently colored chips, and each table has its own set of chips with a unique design that can only be used on that table.*

# PLACING BETS

Players have a wide range of bets from which to choose. The highest paying bet is to predict which number the ball will land in. Since there are 38 numbers on the wheel, this is also the most risky type of bet. The bets with the least risk (and the lowest return) are the even chances: bets on whether the ball will land on red or black, or on an odd or even, high or low number.

Although the betting layout looks complicated, placing bets is quite simple. To bet on individual numbers, the chip is placed directly on top of the number. For two adjacent numbers on the layout, placing a chip on the middle of the line that divides them makes the bet. A bet on red or black, high or low, even or odd is made by placing a chip in the corresponding box on the betting layout.

Casinos use both left- and right-hand tables, which adds to the confusion of placing bets. On a right-hand table, the first column is the one furthest from the dealer; on a left-hand table, it is closest to the dealer. Some basic bets are illustrated opposite. The color in brackets refers to the appropriate chip on the diagram.

## STRAIGHT UP (Green)

This is a bet on any one of the 38 numbers including 0 and 00. The chip should be placed directly on top of the desired number on the layout, ensuring that it is not touching any of the surrounding lines. It wins only if that number is spun. Odds paid are 35 to 1.

## SPLIT (Pink)

A bet on two adjacent numbers on the layout. The bet is placed on the center of the line between the two numbers. It wins if either of the two numbers is spun. Odds paid are 17 to 1 (also written as 17/1).

## STREET (Brown)

A bet on three adjacent numbers across the layout. It wins if any of the numbers is spun. Odds paid are 11/1.

## CORNER (Orange)

A bet on four adjacent numbers on the layout. The chip is placed on the line where they meet. It wins if any of the four numbers is spun. Odds paid are 8 to 1.

## FIRST FOUR (Red)

A bet on the numbers 0, 1, 2, and 3. It is placed on the corner of the layout where 1 and 0 meet. It wins if any of the four numbers win. Odds of 8 to 1 are paid.

## FIRST FIVE (Dark blue)

On a double-zero table, a bet on 0, 00, 1, 2, and 3. It is placed on the lines where 0, 00, and 2 meet. It wins if any of these numbers are spun. Odds paid are 6 to 1.

## DOUBLE STREET (Purple)

A bet on six adjacent numbers across the layout. The chip is placed on the double line at the side of the layout at the cross section of the middle line of the six numbers. Odds paid are 5 to 1.

## QUATRO (Not shown)

Some layouts incorporate bets on a quarter of the numbers. The first quarter is numbers 1–9 inclusive, the second 10–18, the third 19–27, and the fourth 28–36. Bets are placed in the appropriate box. Odds paid are 3 to 1. Bets lose if 0 is spun.

## COLUMN (Black and gray stripes)

A bet on a group of 12 numbers running in one of the three columns along the table. Bets are placed in the box at the base of the column. The bet wins if any number in the column is spun. Odds paid are 2 to 1. All bets on the column lose if 0 is spun.

## DOZEN (Yellow)

A bet on a group of 12 consecutive numbers. There are three dozens: 1–12, 13–24, and 25–36 inclusive. Bets are placed in the appropriate box. The bet wins if any of the 12 numbers is spun. Odds paid are 2 to 1. All bets on the dozens lose if 0 is spun.

## EVEN CHANCE BETS (Magenta and Blue)

Also called the outside bets, these are bets on a certain characteristic of the number spun, such as whether it is red or black, even or odd, high or low. Bets are placed in boxes marked with that characteristic and win if the appropriate characteristic is spun. Odds paid are evens. If 0 or 00 is spun, players lose half their stake.

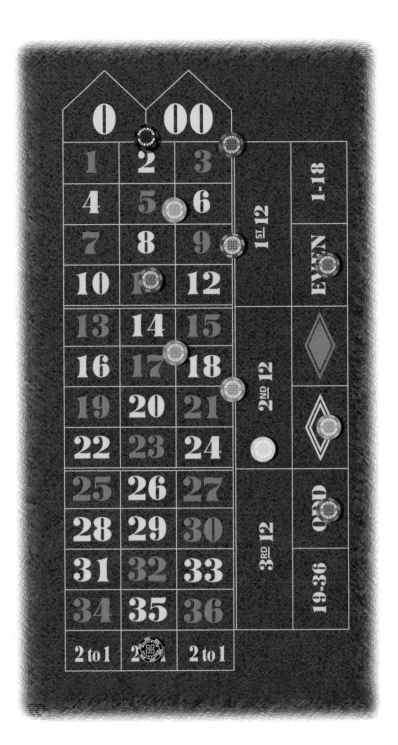

*Bets on dozens are paid at 2 to 1.*

*Even chance bets are paid at 1 to 1.*

ABOVE *Some of the most popular bets on roulette are illustrated in this layout and described in the text opposite. Different color chips have been used to indicate which bet is being shown. When a number of players are betting simultaneously, the layout can become very crowded with chips, making it hard to see where the numbers are situated.*

*A winning column is paid at 2 to 1.*

# PLAYING THE GAME

Before starting to play roulette, players first need to buy table chips. These can be purchased with money, cash chips or, in some casinos, with a personal check. Although bets may be placed using cash chips or money, it is advisable to always take a color, so that your bets are not confused with another player's bets.

The value of the color chips will be marked on the table. The chips are stacked in piles of 20. Each set of color comprises 200 chips. To prove that there are 20 chips in each stack, the dealer will cut the chips down into four piles of five chips, and spread out one of the piles. The dealer will push the chips across the table and leave them in front of you.

When you arrive at the table, there will probably be a game in progress. The best time to buy chips is when the dealer announces "place your bets." Put your money or cash chips in front of you on the table and say "colour." If you want to cash a check, inform the

dealer. Never place money or cash chips for buying color directly on the layout, as it will be assumed that you are making a bet. The dealer will take your money, count it, and pass you the appropriate number of chips. If you have a preference for a particular color, you may ask for it, as long as no other player is using it already. You can then begin betting.

Take care when placing bets. You may intend to bet straight up, but if your chip is touching the line, it may be assumed that it is a split. If other players have already placed bets on the numbers you want, simply put your chip on top of theirs. Never move another player's chips. If a player's bet is badly placed and you want to bet on that number, inform the dealer, who will query the bet with the other player.

When a game gets really busy. it can become difficult to see the numbers as they are all covered in chips. If you are not sure where a number is, ask the dealer to place your bet. Simply place your chip in front of you on the table and announce loudly and clearly what you want to bet on. The dealer will repeat your instructions and place the bet on your behalf.

When the players are almost finished placing bets, the dealer will spin the ball. The starting point of the spin is the last number spun. The first spin of the day is spun from the date. So on July 6, the first spin of the ball will be from number six. If the table is very busy, the dealer will make a long spin. On a quieter table, the spin will be shorter. Players may request a long or short spin (if several players have different preferences the highest staking player usually takes precedence). Some casinos alternate the spin between clockwise and anticlockwise turns to make it less likely that the ball will land in the same area of the wheel.

Occasionally a no-spin will be announced if the ball makes fewer than three revolutions, or if the dealer makes a mistake in spinning the ball. The dealer will attempt to catch the ball, but if he or she misses and the ball happens to land in a number, it will not count as a winning number. The ball will be replaced in the last position and respun.

A short while before the ball drops into the wheel, the dealer will announce "no more bets," and any bets placed after this may be refused. In practice, many players continue betting right until the ball drops, but it is preferable to place bets early on.

Once the ball has settled, the dealer announces the winning number, winning color, and whether it is odd or even. A marker, called a dolly, is placed on top of the chips on the winning number. All losing bets are cleared away. Occasionally, winning bets are removed in error. If this happens, tell the dealer, who will then summon the inspector. As the action on the tables is recorded, any claims can easily be verified.

Winning bets are paid out in a set order, starting with the winning column, even chances, and winning dozen. Then the bets around the number are paid.

*OPPOSITE TOP Chips are normally kept in stacks of 20. To prove that there are 20 chips, the dealer will cut each stack into four piles of five chips, and lay one pile out as singles.*

*LEFT Depending on how busy the table is, the dealer can make either a long or a short spin of the wheel.*

One player may have several winning bets. These will be totaled and paid together.

For each color, the dealer will announce the number of chips won and prepare the payout. The dealer judges how many color chips the player needs to continue playing and will make up the rest of the payout with cash chips. Players can request to have their payout made up however they like.

If you need more color chips or more cash chips, tell the dealer. If you want to stop playing, ask for cash chips. Always check your payout, as mistakes can be made. Queries should be addressed to the inspector.

If zero is spun, the bets associated with zero are paid out as normal, but half of the stake from the even chances is lost and will be removed by the dealer.

When all the bets have been paid out, the dealer will remove the dolly and announce "place your bets." This is the cue to start betting again. All winning bets are left in place, so if you do not want to bet on the same number again you must remove the chip yourself.

*BELOW The dealer places a marker, called a dolly, on top of the winning chips so that they are not swept away in error.*

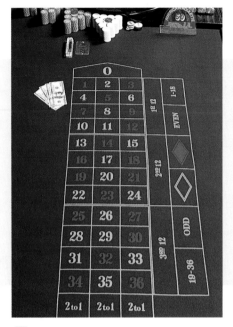

**1** PLAYER PLACES MONEY, OR CASH CHIPS, ON THE TABLE AND CALLS FOR COLOR.

**2** DEALER COUNTS THE MONEY OR CASH CHIPS, AND PASSES THE PLAYER THE APPROPRIATE NUMBER OF TABLE CHIPS.

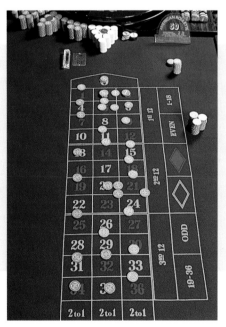

**3** DEALER ANNOUNCES "PLACE YOUR BETS." WHEN BETS ARE PLACED, DEALER SPINS BALL AND ANNOUNCES "NO MORE BETS."

**4** NUMBER 20 WINS. DEALER ANNOUNCES "TWENTY, BLACK, EVEN," AND PLACES A MARKER (DOLLY) ON 20.

**5** DEALER CLEARS AWAY LOSING BETS AND CALCULATES THE WINNING PAYOUTS.

**6** ONE PLAYER HAS A WINNING BET STRAIGHT UP, A SPLIT, A CORNER, AND A DOUBLE STREET. THESE ARE TOTALED, GIVING 65 CHIPS.

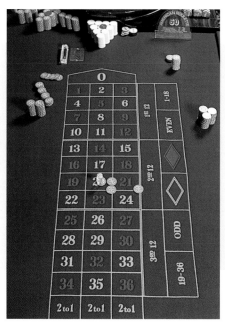

**7** DEALER PROVES THE PAYOUT BY CUTTING DOWN A STACK AND SPREADING THE OTHER FIVE CHIPS.

**8** THE WINNING CHIPS ARE PASSED TO THE PLAYER. THE DEALER ANNOUNCES "PLACE YOUR BETS."

# FRENCH ROULETTE

French roulette, the predecessor of the American version, is mostly played in European casinos and is dealt in French. Although the equipment and language used differs, it is in principle the same game as American roulette, although it is played more slowly.

French roulette is played on a table roughly twice the size of that used for American roulette. The betting layout differs, the numbers are arranged in a random order, and there is only one zero. Each table has two dealers and a *chef de table* (inspector), who are seated around the wheel. The dealers move the chips around using a long stick, called a rake. Players bet by throwing their chips to roughly the correct place, and the dealers then line them up using the rake.

Although the game is dealt in French, players familiar with American roulette can get by with just a few words of French (see Game Speak on page 53).

ABOVE *Monte Carlo Casino is one of many European casinos that offer the French version of roulette.*

RIGHT *The French wheel has a different arrangement of numbers to the American wheel and only one zero. Speciality bets cover particular sections of the wheel.*

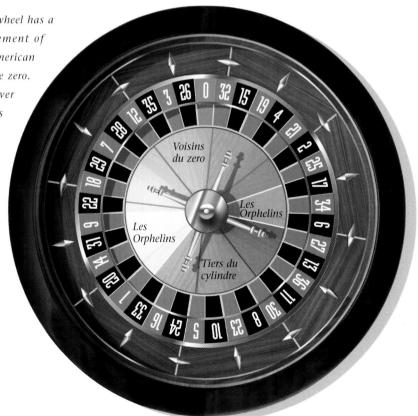

# SPECIALITY BETS

Unlike American roulette, some of the bets placed on French roulette cover particular sections of the wheel.

### TIERS DU CYLINDRE

Commonly called *tiers*. A six-chip bet consisting of splits covering numbers 5/8, 10/11, 13/16, 23/24, 27/30, 33/36. This bet covers almost one third of the wheel, from 33 to 27. If any number in that section is spun, 17 chips are won, and five chips are lost.

### VOISINS DU ZÉRO (illustrated below)

A nine-chip bet that covers the section of the wheel around zero. The bets placed are 0/2/3 (2 chips) street. Splits on 4/7, 12/15, 18/21, 19/22, 32/35, and a four-number bet 25/26/28/29 (2 chips). If 0, 2, 3, 25, 26, 28, or 29 are spun, 16 chips are won and 8 lost. If any other number is spun, 17 chips are won and 8 are lost.

### VOISINS (NEIGHBOR BET)

A bet on five numbers straight up that are adjacent to one another on the wheel. A bet on *cinq et les voisins* (five and the neighbors) is a bet on number 5 and the two numbers either side of it on the wheel (a straight up on 23, 10, 5, 24, and 16). The dealer places these bets. Simply give five chips and announce your bet.

### LES ORPHELINS (illustrated below)

*Les Orphelins* or The Orphans, covers the sections of the wheel that are not covered by the *tiers* and the *voisins du zero*. It is a five-chip bet on number 1 straight and the splits 6/9, 14/17, 17/20, 31/34. If 1 is spun, 35 chips are won and 3 chips lost. However, if number 17 wins, then 34 chips are won, and 3 chips are lost. If either 6, 9, 14, 20, 31, or 34 are spun, 17 chips are won, and 4 chips are lost.

# ENGLISH ROULETTE

This is a hybrid of American and French roulette. To confuse matters, the English call it American roulette. It is mostly played in British and European casinos on American roulette tables using the French wheel (with one zero). The game is played in the same manner as American roulette, but incorporates many elements of French roulette, including French terms for the bets and the speciality bets of *voisins*, *tiers*, and *orphelins*.

## NEIGHBORS OVAL

Some English roulette tables incorporate a neighbors oval. This is a diagram of the wheel printed on the layout in front of the dealer. It allows neighbor bets *(voisins)* to be placed quickly without the difficulty of placing the individual straight-up bets *(en plein)*.

The dealer places the neighbors bets. Simply give the dealer five chips and announce your bet. For "five and the neighbors," the dealer will place the chips on the number 5 on the oval. The ball is spun and the dolly placed as usual. Before clearing the layout, the dealer will point to the winning number on the oval and announce either "neighbors win" or "neighbors lose." If there is a winning neighbor bet, one of the chips is removed from the oval, placed on the winning number, and paid out as a winning straight-up bet.

RIGHT *The neighbors oval enables* voisins *bets to be placed effectively. Not all English tables have one.*

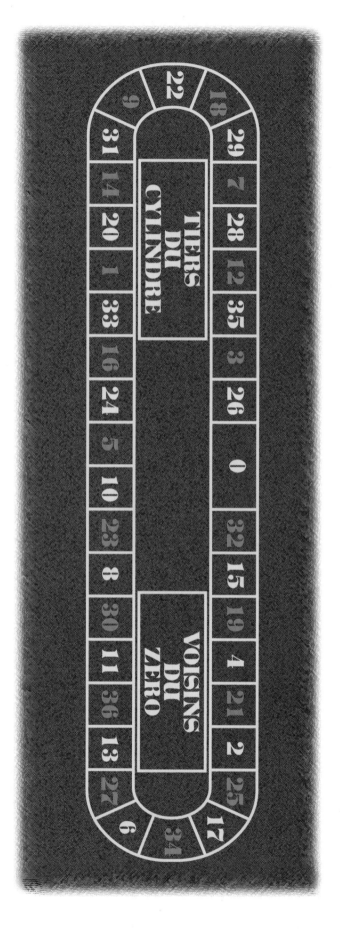

ABOVE *The roulette table at Monte Carlo is given the Expressionist treatment in this early 20th-century painting by Norwegian artist, Edvard Munch.*

# Game Speak

*Carré* – Corner

*Cheval* – Split

*D* – Third/last dozen

*En plein* – Straight up

*Faites vos jeux* – Place your bets

*Impair/Pair* – Odd/Even

*M* – Second/middle dozen

*Manqué* – Low

*P* – First dozen

*Passé* – High

*Quatro* – A bet on a group of nine consecutive numbers

*Rien ne va plus* – No more bets

*Sixainne* – Double street

*Transversale simple* – Street

*Voisin* – Neighbor bet

*Stack* – 20 chips

*Dolly* – marker used on roulette to show the winning number

*Colour* – table chips used on roulette

# SPIN AND WIN

Apart from roulette, there are other casino games that are played using spinning wheels. These echo the original fairground wheel of fortune that is the forerunner of today's mechanical games. They are all games of chance, relying more on luck than on skill.

## BOULE

Boule is found mostly in French and Swiss casinos. Like roulette, players bet where a ball will land on a spinning wheel. Instead of being divided into sections, the boule wheel has a series of indentations which are marked with four sets of the numbers one to nine. The ball used is much larger than that on roulette. Bets include single numbers *(en plein),* the colors red and black, high and low numbers, and even and odd numbers. The number five has the same role as the zero on roulette. If five is spun, then the bets on the outside chances lose. The outside chances are paid at evens and the *en pleins* at seven to one. One of the disadvantages of boule is that the house advantage is so high (11.11 percent as opposed to 2.7 percent on French roulette).

## BIG SIX WHEEL

Big six wheel recalls the game that used to be played at fairs and sideshows, but has now been adapted for casinos. It is a simple game, played with a large spinning wheel which stands vertically and is spun by the dealer. Almost any number of players can participate. The wheel is covered with symbols and payout amounts. The aim is to predict where the wheel will stop. The betting layout is marked with boxes that correspond with the sections of the wheel. Bets are made by placing chips in the relevant number box. In Australia, a similar game is called big money wheel.

ABOVE RIGHT *Roll up and place your bets! Everyone has a chance to win on the spinning wheel, a remnant of the fairground games enjoyed by our grandparents.*

## KENO

Keno is basically a continual lottery. It is popular in American casinos, with many games played each day. Players choose from one to 20 numbers, which they mark onto a ticket or card. They present their ticket to a keno writer along with the appropriate stake, and are issued with a computerized ticket. For each game, 20 numbers are randomly drawn and displayed on boards around the casino. The payouts for different combinations of numbers are also displayed. Players simply need to look at the board and check their ticket to find out if they have a win for the game they played.

Keno is played for small stakes but potentially huge jackpots. An example of this is the 1998 win, at Burswood Casino in Australia, by a woman who won a jackpot totaling A$1 million by selecting 10 out of 10 correct numbers for a A$2 bet.

Games like keno prove that it is not always the good gamblers who win lots of money. An Australian from Townsville who won the biggest keno jackpot in Queensland did so without picking a single winning number. He had played two "quick picks" at a local hotel. Simply because none of his 40 numbers came up, he won A$250,000.

# SLOTS

Slot machines or slots are by far the easiest and most popular casino games to play, because they require no skill on the part of the players. They also offer potentially huge returns for a small investment. There is an almost infinite variety of machines, with new designs constantly being developed. Most mimic traditional fruit machines, with basic symbols on spinning drums—but instead of the original three drums, many now incorporate five drums, or payout lines, making it harder for players to win. Each coin played brings a new line into play, so it makes sense to play the maximum number of lines per spin. Mechanical systems, which used rotating drums and were activated by pulling a lever, have given way to push-button operated, microprocessor-controlled machines with payouts controlled by computer chips, but there is no changing the popularity of the slots.

The object of playing the slots is to spin the drums so that identical symbols end up across the winning line (either vertically or horizontally). There is a hierarchy of symbols, with some giving higher payouts than others. There are also differences in the way the payouts are calculated. Some slots (known as flat-top slots) have set payouts; while the payouts on progressive slots (groups of machines linked by computers) change all the time as more money is played on them. Whenever any of the linked machines are played the overall jackpot increases.

Progressive slots often give huge payouts—often enough to create instant millionaires. In some countries, all the casinos belonging to a group have electronically linked their slots, creating more opportunities for winning megajackpots, regardless of which casino you are playing in. Slots can pay out up to 98 percent of the money put into them, but of course, this does not mean that an individual player will win 98 percent of the time. Large payouts may only happen once or twice a year, leaving the majority of players to share the balance in the form of small returns.

RIGHT *Slot machines are the casino's mainstay, offering the chance of instant riches to the lucky few.*

ABOVE *Banks of slot machines are often linked to a progressive jackpot, which increases every time a machine is played. The running total encourages players to take a chance—as the big win could be just one coin away.*

Instructions for playing are printed on every slot machine, together with the relevant payout odds. Small amounts are paid out directly by the machines. However, if a large jackpot is won, it will be paid by a member of the casino's staff, who will be notified of the win by a flashing light over the machine.

Slots are traditionally played using either coins or metal tokens, which are purchased at the cash point. Coinless slots are becoming increasingly popular nowadays, and many new establishments—such as Sun International's GrandWest Casino in Cape Town, South Africa—are dispensing with coins altogether in favor of cards. A voucher or smart card (which looks like a credit card) is purchased, and can then be used on all the slot machines in that casino.

Card-based systems have resulted in the creation of loyalty programs for regular customers, who can build up points which can be exchanged for comps such as accommodation, meals, or beverages.

Latest innovations are adventure-style video slots based on arcade games. State-of-the-art computer graphics and cutting-edge technology create realistic

images, sound, and animation, while fantasy designs encourage players to move from one machine to the next in the hope of hitting the jackpot.

There are also video slots that imitate table games like poker, blackjack, and roulette. These are popular with less confident players, as they allow one-on-one betting against the machine, instead of placing bets at a crowded table.

For casinos, slots are extremely profitable, despite the large percentage return that is paid out in winnings. In recent years, they have accounted for more than 60 percent of the total gaming turnover in Nevada, which has over 120,000 slot machines, most of them in Las Vegas. It is estimated that almost 70 percent of visitors to Atlantic City casinos play the slots.

ABOVE *Microchip-controlled smart cards represent the future of gaming, dispensing with the need for coins, but does this mean the end of the noisy gaming floor?*

LEFT *Video poker allows players to bet on a standard five-card hand, with options to hold cards or deal new ones in order to make the best possible ranking.*

# BLACKJACK

*Where it pays to count your cards*

BLACKJACK, which is based on the card game 21, or pontoon, is one of the most popular table games due to the fact that players do not have to rely on luck alone. Instead, it is the way they play that determines whether they win or lose. Computer simulations that have calculated the best strategies for winning demonstrate that it is possible to overcome the casino's advantage. To achieve this means memorizing the best action to take, depending on the cards that are dealt—but players who master the skill have a realistic chance of winning.

Blackjack is played against the dealer, who plays on the casino's behalf. The aim is to draw cards that will beat the dealer's hand without exceeding a score of 21. Standard decks of 52 cards are used (jokers are not used), and the number of decks does not affect the game. Six decks are most often used, giving a total of 312 cards in play.

RIGHT *The object of the game is to beat the dealer by making the closest score to 21.*

LEFT *"Blackjack" is an ace plus any other card that has a face value of 10 (king, queen, jack, or 10).*

ABOVE *A blackjack table can accommodate up to seven people. As with other table games, the colored chips are unique to each table and cannot be used elsewhere in the casino.*

Blackjack is played on a semicircular table, which is operated by a dealer who shuffles and deals the cards, pays out winning bets, and collects losing bets. There are places for up to seven players (see left). A player may play more than one hand at a time, with each hand counting as a separate bet against the dealer.

Although some casinos use machines, the cards are mostly shuffled by hand. After shuffling, the dealer will invite a player to cut the cards by inserting a blank card about one deck from the end of the shoe from which the cards are dealt. To deter card counters, a card is removed (burned or killed) from the top of the deck and placed in the discard pile. Players are not allowed to touch the cards (this is to stop cards from being switched, removed, or marked by cheats).

Players start by making an initial bet. One card is then dealt face up to each player and face down to the dealer, followed by a second card dealt face up to each player as well as to the dealer. The players add up the value of the cards they hold and try to assess the potential score of the dealer's hand before making their next moves. The objective is to achieve a total closer to 21 than the dealer's cards, but not to exceed 21 (in which case the player loses). The skill lies in trying to work out the probabilities of that occurring.

ABOVE *A shuffled pack is cut by inserting a blank card into the deck to indicate when it should be reshuffled.*

Blackjack, the highest hand possible, is an ace plus any card worth 10. Only the first two cards dealt can make blackjack. Cards dealt to a split hand do not count.

## SCORING

The card values in each player's hand are added to give the scores. Cards from 2–10 inclusive have their face value. Court cards (kings, queens, and jacks) are worth 10. Aces have an initial value of 11, decreasing to 1 if the hand subsequently exceeds a score of 21.

## WHERE TO PLACE BETS

Players may bet on as many boxes as they wish. They have the option of playing themselves or, in Europe and some other countries, betting on another player's hand. This is useful if you are a novice and not yet confident of your own skills.

The second player bets by placing their chip next to the original bet. The first player has complete control over the hand and all action taken. If a hand is split (see next page) the second player does not have to make an additional bet, but may nominate which hand he or she wishes to bet on. Similarly, the second player does not have to double if the original player doubles.

*Queen (10) & ace (11) is blackjack (21).*

*King (10) & 10 give a score of 20.*

*7 & 8 give a score of 15.*

*Ace (11) & 8 is 19. If a 2 is dealt, this becomes 21.*

# BEGINNING THE GAME

After making their initial bets by placing chips in the boxes marked on the table, the players are dealt two cards face up. The dealer also receives two cards, only one of which is revealed (the up card). The dealer's other card (the hole card) remains face down.

After assessing the value of their hand, players can choose from several options —depending on the value of his or her own hand and the dealer's up card—to enable them to beat the dealer without going over 21.

**Options for play:** Some of the actions a player can take are shown in the illustration above.

• **Stand** (Green chip) Take no further cards

• **Hit** (Purple chip) Take one or more cards to improve their score. The procedure for asking for another card varies. In the U.S.A., it is common practice to tap the table to hit (take another card) and to wave your hand (or move it horizontally) to pass (not accept another card). In the U.K., the dealer will ask each player in turn if he or she wants another card, and the player simply replies "yes" or "no." In the event of a dispute or mis-understanding, players should refer to the inspector.

• **Split** (Red chips) Normally occurs when the first two cards are the same (for example two 9s). The player splits the hand by placing an additional bet on the line of the box. With aces, only one more card may be dealt to each hand, but on any other split, players can draw as many cards as required. Some casinos allow a split hand to be resplit. Splits can only score 21, not black-jack.

• **Double** (Blue chips) Under certain conditions players may double their bet by increasing it to twice the initial stake. Despite the name, players do not have to double the initial stake, but may make an additional bet up to the total value of the initial bet.

Doubling is usually restricted to the first two cards dealt, and players are then allowed only one further card to each hand. The double bet is made by placing chips behind the original bet after the first two cards are dealt to a player's hand. Winning bets are paid at odds of evens. The rules for doubling vary in different casinos, and players should enquire before making this type of bet. After a player doubles, a third card is dealt and its value is added to the first two cards.

Doubling is also known as buying another card.

If a player's score exceeds 21 at any time, he or she loses, and the dealer clears away the cards. Even if the dealer's hand exceeds 21, the player still loses, but this is not counted as a standoff (a tie between the dealer and a player).

Players stand (take no more cards) when they are satisfied they have sufficient cards to beat the dealer's eventual score. When all the players have indicated that they are standing, the dealer plays his or her hand by revealing the down card (also called the hole card).

The casino has set rules that determine the action to be taken by the dealer based on the total of the two cards. If the dealer's cards add up to 17 or over, he or she must stand. With a score of 16 or less, the dealer must take additional cards until the total exceeds 16. If the dealer's score goes above 21, the house loses (goes bust), and the players' winning bets are paid out.

If the dealer's score is below 21, players with higher scores win and are paid out. If the score is a standoff (a tie) on blackjack or any other total, the bet is not lost, and the player's original stake is returned.

When a player is dealt blackjack, and it is obvious that the dealer cannot make blackjack (the dealer's up card is any value from 2–9), the player's winnings are paid out, and his or her cards are removed before any further cards are dealt to the other players.

However, if the dealer's up card is an ace or any card with a value of 10, the player with blackjack waits until all the other players' hands are played. This is necessary because the dealer may have blackjack and therefore tie with the player. The outcome for the player with blackjack will only be determined when the dealer's down card is revealed.

## ODDS PAID

Payouts are calculated according to the value of the player's hand when compared with the dealer's hand. If a player has blackjack and beats the dealer, the odds paid are 3 to 2. A win pays even money. A standoff results in the original stake being returned.

If a player has taken insurance (see next) against the dealer making blackjack, the insurance bet will be paid out at 2 to 1 if this occurs.

## INSURANCE

If the dealer's first card is an ace, he or she will ask the players if they want to take insurance. This is an additional bet, equal to half of the player's original stake, against the possibility of the dealer making blackjack. If the dealer subsequently does make blackjack, the original bet loses, but the insurance bet is paid at odds of 2 to 1. If the dealer does not have blackjack, the insurance bet is lost and the original bet is paid out at 3 to 2. Whatever the outcome of the dealer's hand, the net result is the same; even money is won.

If a player takes insurance, most casinos immediately pay out the bet at evens and remove the player's cards. Taking insurance is not generally considered a good bet as the dealer's chances of making blackjack are outweighed by the chance of making other scores.

## ADDITIONAL BETS

Some casinos have introduced additional bets on blackjack. However, they do not really offer good value, and novices will find that it is better to concentrate on learning how to play the basic game well.

**Surrender blackjack**  If a player is dealt a poor initial hand, he or she may surrender half of his or her stake, which is removed by the dealer, and the player's hand is not played. However, if the dealer has blackjack the entire stake is lost.

**Over/under 13**  This is simply a bet that the first two cards dealt will be either over or under 13. The additional bet loses if the score is exactly 13. This bet is placed at the same time as the initial bet. Whatever the outcome of the additional bet, the hand is played out as normal.

**Multiple action blackjack**  The player keeps the same hand for three games, and the dealer the same up card. The first two cards are dealt as norma, and the player may draw on these cards. The dealer follows the normal rules for drawing cards (stands on 17 or over, draws on 16 or under). A good hand has the chance of winning three times over but, conversely, a bad hand could lose three times in succession.

**Three 7s**  This is a bet on being dealt three 7s, and can be made at the same time as the initial bet.

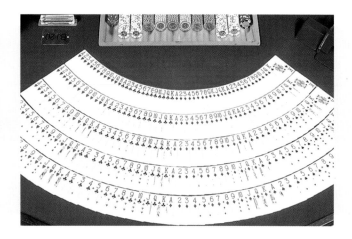

**1** BEFORE THE DAY'S PLAY BEGINS, THE DEALER FANS OUT THE DECKS OF CARDS IN NUMERICAL SEQUENCE, SUIT BY SUIT, TO CHECK THAT FULL DECKS ARE BEING USED.

THE CARDS ARE ALSO SCRUTINIZED TO ENSURE THAT THEY ARE NOT MARKED OR DAMAGED IN ANY WAY. ALL MARKED CARDS ARE REMOVED AND REPLACED IMMEDIATELY. THIS APPLIES THROUGHOUT PLAY.

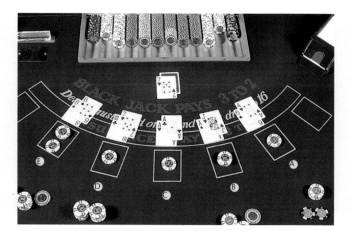

**2** THE ORDER OF PLAY IS FROM THE DEALER'S LEFT (THAT IS FROM RIGHT TO LEFT IN THE ILLUSTRATIONS).

PLAYERS PLACE THEIR INITIAL BETS IN THE BOXES MARKED ON THE LAYOUTS. TWO PLAYERS ARE BETTING ON BOX E. THE SECOND PLAYER PLACES HIS BET BELOW THE FIRST PLAYER'S CHIP.

TWO CARDS ARE THEN DEALT FACE UP TO EACH PLAYER.

THE DEALER RECEIVES TWO CARDS (ONE CARD FACE UP AND THE OTHER CARD, CALLED THE HOLE CARD, FACE DOWN).

**3** PLAYER A HAS A SCORE OF 10 (6 + 4).

PLAYER B HAS BLACKJACK (ACE + JACK) AND IS PAID OUT IMMEDIATELY AT 3:2 AS THE DEALER'S UP CARD CARD (7) SHOWS IT IS NOT POSSIBLE TO SCORE BLACKJACK.

PLAYER C HAS A SCORE OF 12 (FIRST ACE = 11, 2ND ACE = 1).

PLAYER D HAS A SCORE OF 17.

PLAYER E HAS A SCORE OF 14.

**4** PLAYERS MAY NOW TAKE EXTRA CARDS.

PLAYER A HITS (CALLS FOR ANOTHER CARD) AND IS DEALT A 10, GIVING A TOTAL SCORE OF 20.

PLAYER A DECIDES TO STAND ON THAT SCORE.

**5** PLAYER C DECIDES TO SPLIT. EACH ACE NOW BECOMES THE FIRST CARD ON TWO SEPARATE HANDS, WITH A VALUE OF 11.
EACH NEW HAND IS DEALT ONE MORE CARD. THE FIRST HAND SCORES 17 (11 + 6) AND THE OTHER 21 (11 + 10). THIS IS NOT BLACKJACK, AS IT HAS BEEN MADE WITH A SPLIT HAND.

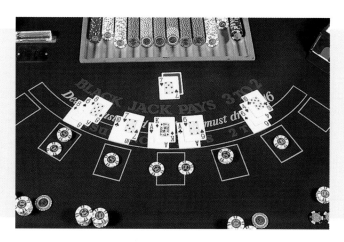

**6** PLAYER D DECIDES TO STAND ON HIS SCORE OF 17.
PLAYER E HITS (TAKES ANOTHER CARD) AND DRAWS AN 8, TO END UP WITH A TOTAL OF 22.
THIS IS CALLED A BUST, AS THE VALUE OF HIS CARDS EXCEEDS 21.

**7** THE DEALER REMOVES PLAYER E'S STAKE AND CARDS.
THE REMAINING PLAYERS ALL DECIDE TO STAND.

**8** THE DEALER'S SECOND CARD IS REVEALED AS A KING, GIVING THE DEALER A SCORE OF 17.
PLAYER A HAS A HIGHER SCORE (20) THAN THE DEALER, SO WINS AND IS PAID ODDS OF EVENS.
PLAYER C HAS ONE HAND WITH THE SAME SCORE AS THE DEALER. AS THIS IS A STANDOFF (A TIE) HE KEEPS HIS STAKE. THE OTHER HAND BEATS THE DEALER AND IS PAID AT ODDS OF EVENS.
PLAYER D ALSO HAS A STANDOFF AND KEEPS THE STAKE.

ABOVE *Blackjack tables await players in the elegant and traditional Monte Carlo Casino.*

# BASIC STRATEGY

Blackjack is a game where a player's individual skills can have an effect on his or her winnings. The average house advantage on blackjack is 5.6 percent but there are ways that players can overcome this.

Using computer programs to simulate games a system, known as basic strategy, has been developed which determines the best action for players to take according to the value of the cards they hold.

By playing basic strategy players can reduce the house advantage to zero. This involves memorizing the correct action to take for the cards dealt. In its simplest form, basic strategy means hitting on a score of 16 or lower if the dealer shows a 7 or above, and standing on a score of 12 or higher if the dealer shows 6 or lower. The chart below shows basic strategy in more detail. It takes time to memorize, but is worth studying if you intend to play blackjack seriously.

| PLAYER'S HAND | DEALER'S UP CARD | | | | | | | | | |
|---|---|---|---|---|---|---|---|---|---|---|
| | 2 | 3 | 4 | 5 | 6 | 7 | 8 | 9 | 10 | Ace |
| 8 | H | H | H | H | H | H | H | H | H | H |
| 9 | H | D | D | D | D | H | H | H | H | H |
| 10 | D | D | D | D | D | D | D | D | H | H |
| 11 | D | D | D | D | D | D | D | D | D | H |
| 12 | H | H | X | X | X | H | H | H | H | H |
| 13 | X | X | X | X | X | H | H | H | H | H |
| 14 | X | X | X | X | X | H | H | H | H | H |
| 15 | X | X | X | X | X | H | H | H | H | H |
| 16 | X | X | X | X | X | H | H | H | H | H |
| 17 | X | X | X | X | X | X | X | X | X | X |
| 18 | X | X | X | X | X | X | X | X | X | X |
| 19 | X | X | X | X | X | X | X | X | X | X |
| 20 | X | X | X | X | X | X | X | X | X | X |
| 21 | X | X | X | X | X | X | X | X | X | X |
| Ace 2 | H | H | H | D | D | H | H | H | H | H |
| Ace 3 | H | H | H | D | D | H | H | H | H | H |
| Ace 4 | H | H | D | D | D | H | H | H | H | H |
| Ace 5 | H | H | D | D | D | H | H | H | H | H |
| Ace 6 | H | D | D | D | D | H | H | H | H | H |
| Ace 7 | X | X | X | X | X | X | X | H | H | H |
| Ace 8 | X | X | X | X | X | X | X | X | X | X |
| Ace 9 | X | X | X | X | X | X | X | X | X | X |
| Ace 10 | X | X | X | X | X | X | X | X | X | X |
| Ace Ace | S | S | S | S | S | S | S | S | S | S |
| 2 2 | S | S | S | S | S | S | S | S | S | S |
| 3 3 | S | S | S | S | S | S | H | H | H | H |
| 4 4 | H | H | H | H | H | H | H | H | H | H |
| 5 5 | D | D | D | D | D | D | D | D | H | H |
| 6 6 | S | S | S | S | S | H | H | H | H | H |
| 7 7 | S | S | S | S | S | S | H | H | H | H |
| 8 8 | S | S | S | S | S | S | S | S | S | X |
| 9 9 | S | S | S | S | S | X | S | S | X | X |
| 10 10 | X | X | X | X | X | X | X | X | X | X |

H = HIT          X = STAND          D = DOUBLE          S = SPLIT

# CARD COUNTING

Another technique for reducing the house advantage is card counting, which gives players a chance of beating the casino. The house advantage on blackjack is given as an average (normally 5.6 percent), because frequent random card shuffling means that the house advantage constantly changes throughout a game.

There are times in a game when the player has an advantage. This arises if more high cards (those with a face value of ten) remain in the shoe than low value cards. When this occurs the dealer is at a disadvantage, due to the rules that determine when he or she must take further cards. Players can stand on any score, but the dealer must hit (take another card) on 16 or lower. Therefore the dealer has a much greater chance of busting if there are plenty of tens left in the shoe. Spotting when this happens is the basis for card counting. The player can then make increased bets knowing that the casino has little chance of winning.

Accomplished card counters can have an advantage of between one and 1.5 percent over the casino if card counting is combined with the basic strategy. Card counting techniques work by assigning a value to each card. As the cards are dealt, players keep a running count, and when a certain level is reached, bets are increased. There are numerous methods that can be used, but the simplest ones are often the best.

Becoming an accomplished card counter takes a lot of practice and complete concentration. Learning to count several cards or whole hands at once improves the speed. It is best to practice at home until the techniques have been mastered.

In the example of card counting shown below, a running count is kept as the cards are dealt. Aces and cards with a face value of 10 are counted as minus one. Cards with a value of two to six inclusive are counted as plus one. When the count is positive, the player begins to increase his bets.

### CARD COUNTING

| | |
|---|---|
| 10 = -1 | 2 = +1 |
| J = -1 | 3 = +1 |
| Q = -1 | 4 = +1 |
| K = -1 | 5 = +1 |
| A = -1 | 6 = +1 |

Using the card counting technique effectively is only half the battle, however. The other challenge is to avoid detection by the casino. Although card counting is not illegal, casinos do everything in their power to deter card counters. Players suspected of card counting are usually asked to leave.

Casinos also try to combat card counters by "burning" cards (dealing a few cards unseen into the discard pile), adding more decks to the shoe, shuffling the cards frequently, and using shuffling machines.

A classic sign of card counting in action is a player making much higher bets in the second half of the shoe. Casino personnel are trained to look out for this and report it to pit bosses. Once spotted, a suspected card counter will be watched, often by the pit boss, but also from the camera room.

LEFT *Blackjack is dealt at high speed so players need to make calculations just as quickly if they want to win.*

If you want to try card counting, the best way to go undetected is to be a small fish in a big pond. If the casino is busy, with lots of high rollers playing, all the attention will be on them and a player betting small stakes may be overlooked. Limiting the length of sessions means a player is less likely to be remembered. Avoid high denomination chips as these will attract attention. Put your winning chips in a bag or pocket, not on the table, and exchange them at the cash point at frequent intervals.

If the pit boss starts watching you, then continue playing normally for low stakes. The pit boss regularly checks each table's float. If you've suddenly won a lot of money, make yourself scarce. The inspector may not notice you winning small amounts, but the pit boss will realize this once the float is counted.

To evade detection, professional card counters work in a team and enter the casino separately. One player starts playing blackjack for low stakes and counts the cards. The other members of the team wait for a signal from the player that the shoe favors the players and

when it is given, the other team members quickly join the game and start playing for high stakes. This technique can only safely be used once in a casino, as the players will be identified and a record kept of their big wins. If the same group returns and wins again, the casino staff may quickly become suspicious.

ABOVE *Frequent shuffling by hand or machine is just one of the methods casinos use to deter card counters.*

# *Game Speak*

*Anchor box* – the player who is dealt cards first is sitting on the anchor box (see also First base)

*Basic strategy* – a playing strategy in blackjack that reduces the house advantage

*Blackjack* – traditionally a score of 21 made with an ace and the jack of spades or clubs, now more commonly an ace plus any card worth 10

*Break* – a score over 21

*Burned cards* – cards discarded by the dealer without being seen by the players

*Bust* – to achieve a score over 21 (to go bust)

*Card counting* – an advanced technique for reducing the house advantage

*Cut card* – a blank card used for cutting the deck, to show when the cards must be reshuffled

*Draw* – to take another card

*First base* – the player who is dealt cards first

*Hard hand* – a score of 12 or more

*Heads up* – playing alone at a table

*Hit* – to take another card

*Hole card* – the dealer's face down card

*Natural* – a hand that scores 21 with the first two cards dealt

*Pair* – two cards of the same value

*Pass* – to take no further cards

*Push* – a bet that is tied

*Sabot* – box where cards are placed for dealing

*Shoe* – box where cards are placed for dealing

*Soft hand* – a score of 11 or less, meaning a card can be drawn without busting

*Stand* – to take no more cards

*Standoff* – a tie with the dealer

*Stiff hand* – a score of 12 – 16

*Up card* – the dealer's face up card

# DICE GAMES

*It's a natural for the shooter*

THE rowdiest game in the casino is dice, also called craps, a fast and exciting game with a language of its own. Players shout, cheer, scream, curse, and gesticulate. The shooters elaborately shake the dice, blow on them for luck, and yell for them to fall on the desired score, while the stickman commentates incessantly. For novices, dice appears complicated due to the arrangement of the layout and the terminology used, but it is actually quite simple once the basic aim of the game is understood. Craps is extremely popular everywhere, not only because it is fun to play, but also because it is the best value game in the casino. The house advantage on some bets is less than one percent.

Two-up is an Australian coin tossing game which is as noisy as craps. It is not a dice game, but since it involves throwing an object and betting on where it will land, it has been included in this chapter. Two-up is very easy to play. Two coins are thrown into the air and players bet on whether they will land on heads or tails.

RIGHT *Tumbling dice hold craps players in suspense as they wait to see whether the spots will favor them.*

LEFT *A curved stick is used to move chips around the table and collect the dice after they have been thrown.*

Poker, a card game played by four players, is based on the ranking of the hands. The game is played with one standard deck of 52 playing cards. Players aim to win the pot (the money staked) by having the highest ranking five-card hand. When poker is played in a casino, a dealer is provided, and the casino charges the players either an hourly rate or a percentage of the pot (called the rake—typically between five and 10 percent of the pot). There are many variations of poker. Each has different rules about the number of cards dealt and the method of betting, but they all have in common the ranking of the hands and the action that must be taken at every step of the game.

Types of poker played in casinos include five-card draw, seven-card stud, Texas hold 'em, and Omaha. Caribbean poker (also known as casino poker) differs from the other versions in that players play against the casino, not against each other. Games of the same name may be played differently in some casinos, so it is important to check the rules before playing.

The basic action that takes place in a poker game can be summarized as follows:

**Raise**    a bet that players must match or exceed.
**Call**     to bet the same amount as the preceding player in order to remain in the game.
**Fold**     to withdraw from the game and lose all the money you have staked.

At the beginning of each game, the pot is seeded to ensure there is at least some money on the game. Seeding is done in various ways. In some games, before play commences all the players are required to make a bet called an ante, which is usually equivalent to the minimum stake. In others, there are rounds of blind betting in which bets of varying amounts are made before the players look at their hands.

BELOW *Playing poker can be fun, and the thrill of a win enhances even a social game of poker.*

Some casinos may have fixed rules about betting, such as specific amounts that stakes can be raised by (for example, multiples of five), or that a bet or raise must fall within a spread limit (such as any amount between $1 and $5). Players should ensure they are familiar with local systems before getting into a game.

After the cards are dealt, the players can discard and exchange them before a second round of betting takes place. Betting moves clockwise until each player has either called all bets or folded. A showdown then takes place, with each player still in the game revealing his or her cards. The last player to bet is the first to show his or her hand, with the other hands revealed in turn.

Players with losing hands may discard their cards without the other players seeing them, and they will will lose their stakes. The player with the highest ranking hand wins the pot. In a tie, the pot is split equally.

## RANKING OF THE HANDS

A poker hand usually consists of five cards. Aces are the highest ranked cards, followed by kings, queens, and jacks, then the numbers in descending order, with 2s being the lowest. The suits do not affect the rankings. The photographs below and on the next page show the order in which the hands are ranked.

**1. Royal flush** – the best hand, comprising ace, king, queen, jack, and 10 of the same suit.

**2. Straight flush** – five cards of the same suit in consecutive numerical order.

**3. Four of a kind** – four cards of the same value with any other card.

**4. Full house** – three cards of the same value (three of a kind), plus a pair (two cards of the same value). Where two players have a full house, the hand with the highest value for the three of a kind wins.

**5. Flush** – five cards of the same suit in any numerical order. If more than one player has a flush, the hand with the higher cards takes precedence.

**6. Straight** – any five cards in consecutive numerical order, regardless of suit. A, K, Q, J, 10 is the highest, or top straight followed by K, Q, J, 10, 9.

**7. Three of a kind** – three cards of the same value with two cards of different values. If two players have three of a kind, then the player with the highest value cards wins (so K, K, K beats 8, 8, 8).

**8. Two pairs** – two sets of pairs with any other card. If two players both have the same pairs, the highest ranking other card decides who wins. So for example, A, A, 6, 6, 7 beats A, A, 6, 6, 5.

**9. One pair** – two cards of the same value with three cards of different values. If two players have the same pair, the hand with the highest value of other cards wins. So A, A, K, 4, 2 beats A, A, Q, 3, 2.

**10. Highest card** – if none of the above hands is held, the winner is the player with the highest card. So a hand with an ace would beat a hand with a king.

## CHANCES OF MAKING A RANKING HAND

Using a standard deck of 52 cards there are 2,598,960 possible five-card hands that can be dealt. The table below shows the chances and odds of making each ranked hand.

| HAND | NUMBER OF WAYS IT CAN BE MADE WITH FIVE CARDS | ODDS OF MAKING A RANKING HAND FROM THE FIRST FIVE CARDS DEALT |
|---|---|---|
| Royal flush | 4 | 649,739 to 1 |
| Straight flush | 36 | 72,192 to 1 |
| Four of a kind | 624 | 4,164 to 1 |
| Full house | 3,744 | 693 to 1 |
| Flush | 5,108 | 508 to 1 |
| Straight | 10,200 | 254 to 1 |
| Three of a kind | 54,912 | 46 to 1 |
| Two pairs | 123,552 | 20 to 1 |
| One pair | 1,908,240 | 15 to 1 |
| Highest card | 1,302,540 | 1 to 1 |

## BLUFFING

Poker involves more than just betting on the value of a hand. It is also a game of nerve, where players rely not just on the luck of the deal but on their ability to bluff when they have a poor hand. Players constantly scrutinize each other's movements, mannerisms, and facial expressions, trying to judge whether or not their opponents have a good hand or are bluffing.

## JOINING A GAME

On entering a card room there will most probably be a number of games in progress as well as players waiting. New players need to register to get into a game. The player's name will be placed on a list, and he or she will be called as soon as a seat is free at a table. Casino staff will direct players to the appropriate table when their names are called.

Players are not usually allowed to buy chips during the course of a game, so sufficient chips should be purchased beforehand to last for an entire game. All chips must remain on the table throughout the game.

Although the minimum stakes for poker may appear low, a game like draw poker needs chips to the value of about 40 times the minimum stake. Seven-card stud requires about 50 times, while Hold 'em and Omaha need around 100 times the minimum stake. If a player runs out of money (chips) during a game, a second pot will be played for. The player who has no further funds still has a chance to win the first pot, while the other players continue to play for both pots.

## TABLE ETIQUETTE

Players are only allowed to touch their own cards and chips. Everything else on the table is out of bounds. The cards must remain in view at all times (players are not allowed to put cards into a pocket, for example).

Take care when handling your cards. If another player sees them, your hand may be declared dead, and you can take no further part in that game. Dropping cards also results in the hand being declared dead.

Do not throw chips at the pot or at the dealer. Bets are made by placing chips directly in front of you. The dealer will check you have bet the correct amount and put the chips into the pot. It is important to give clear verbal instructions of your action. Call for "time" if you need to make a decision. Players still in a game show this by placing a chip on top of their cards.

The dealer is responsible for dealing the cards, removing losing hands, exchanging money for chips, giving change for large denomination chips, and paying the pot to the winner, who normally tips the dealer.

Players may leave the card table for a short break, during which the dealer will watch your chips. Some rooms specify a time limit for breaks and may allocate the seat to another player if you are gone for too long.

Players can stop playing and leave at the completion of any game. Even if you have won all the chips on a table, you do not have to go on playing and allow the other players to win them back. A new player will be allocated to the table so the game can continue.

Each player receives five cards face down. When all the cards have been dealt, the players look at their own cards. After an initial round of betting, they have the opportunity to exchange any cards in their hand for new cards from the deck. Cards that are being discarded are returned to the dealer before the new cards are drawn.

As a general rule, if you get nothing from the initial deal you should fold (that is, if you are unable to make a ranking of at least a high pair). Only a hand with a pair of at least six or more is worth playing.

The number of cards each player exchanges gives an indication of the strength of his or her hand. A player holding just one pair can improve his or her hand by exchanging up to three cards. However, if three cards are exchanged, the player then makes it obvious that the hand contains a pair. By exchanging only two cards, some doubt remains as to whether the player holds a pair or three of a kind. The extra card retained, which is called a kicker, is usually the highest other card in the hand.

In the illustrations on this page and to follow, the players' cards are not revealed (to duplicate the normal course of play), but are indicated to the reader in the accompanying text. Play moves clockwise around the table, with Player A in the 12-o'clock position, Player B in the 3-o'clock position, and so on.

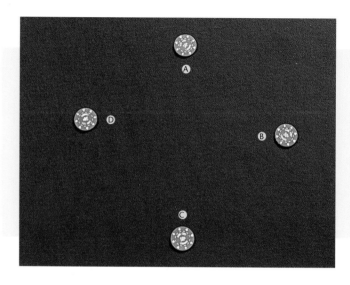

**1** TO START THE GAME, THE POT IS SEEDED. THIS MEANS THAT EACH PLAYER MAKES A BET OF EQUAL VALUE.

**2** FIVE CARDS ARE DEALT FACE DOWN TO EACH PLAYER.

| | | | | |
|---|---|---|---|---|
| PLAYER A HOLDS: 3♦ | 10♦ | 4♠ | 8♠ | 5♣ |
| PLAYER B HOLDS: 9♥ | 9♣ | 10♥ | K♦ | 2♠ |
| PLAYER C HOLDS: 4♥ | 5♥ | 6♣ | 10♠ | K♣ |
| PLAYER D HOLDS: Q♠ | Q♦ | 3♠ | 4♦ | A♣ |

**3** PLAYER A HAS BEEN DEALT NOTHING AND, AS THE CHANCES OF GETTING ONE PAIR FROM EXCHANGING THREE CARDS ARE SLIM, PLAYER A FOLDS. ALL THE MONEY CONTRIBUTED BY PLAYER A TO THE POT IS LOST.

**4** PLAYER B HAS A HIGH PAIR, WHICH IS WORTH PLAYING, AND TAKES TWO CARDS, RETAINING A KICKER. NOW THE OTHER PLAYERS DO NOT KNOW IF ONE PAIR OR THREE OF A KIND ARE HELD, OR IF PLAYER B IS BLUFFING.
PLAYER B'S NEW CARDS: Q♣ 2♦
PLAYER B NOW HOLDS: 9♥ 9♣ K♦ Q♣ 2♦

**5** PLAYER C HAS NOTHING, BUT HAS THE POSSIBILITY OF MAKING A STRAIGHT FLUSH, A FLUSH, OR A STRAIGHT. PLAYER C DRAWS TWO NEW CARDS.
PLAYER D HAS A PAIR OF QUEENS (A HIGH PAIR) AND DECIDES TO TAKE TWO CARDS, RETAINING ONE CARD AS A KICKER.
PLAYER C'S NEW CARDS: 6♠ 7♥
PLAYER D'S NEW CARDS: 8♥ 7♣
PLAYER C NOW HOLDS: 4♥ 5♥ 6♣ 6♠ 7♥
PLAYER D NOW HOLDS: Q♦ Q♠ 8♥ 7♣ A♣

**6** PLAYER B'S HAND IS NOT IMPROVED AFTER THE DRAW, BUT HE STAYS IN THE GAME.
PLAYER C NOW HAS A LOW PAIR AND FOLDS.
PLAYER D'S HAND IS NOT IMPROVED, BUT HE ALSO STAYS IN THE GAME.

**7** IT HAS NOW BECOME A TEST OF NERVE BETWEEN PLAYERS B AND D, AND THEY CONTINUE TO BET.
PLAYER B HAS THE CONFIDENCE TO KEEP RAISING HIS BETS.

**8** THE POT GRADUALLY INCREASES AS BETTING CONTINUES.

**9** PLAYER B HAS SUFFICIENT CONFIDENCE IN HIS HAND TO CONTINUE TO RAISE.
PLAYER D INITIALLY DECIDES TO MATCH PLAYER B, BUT EVENTUALLY HE LOSES HIS NERVE AND FOLDS.

**10** PLAYER B IS THEREFORE THE WINNER AND KEEPS THE POT.
AS PLAYER D HAS FOLDED, PLAYER B DOES NOT HAVE TO REVEAL HIS CARDS.
IN FACT, PLAYER D'S HAND WAS WORTH MORE THAN PLAYER B'S HAND, BUT PLAYER B MANAGED TO FORCE PLAYER D OUT OF THE GAME.

ABOVE *Card games have a long-established reputation for leading unwary players into difficulties. This 1878 etching entitled* The Road to Ruin *seems to depict the result of a long night's gaming.*

Stud poker differs from draw poker in that some of the cards in each player's hand are revealed to the other players. The object of both games remains the same, that is, to beat the other players' hands by making the best ranking poker hand.

To begin, each player receives one card face up and one card face down. The player with the lowest face-up card makes an initial bet, called a forced bet, in order to get the betting started. The remaining three cards are then dealt face up to each player, with a round of betting taking place after each card is dealt. The player showing the highest ranking hand is the first to bet in each remaining round.

As five-card stud progresses, each player gets more information about the other players' hands on which to base his or her subsequent bets. A good initial hand is one that matches or betters the highest card showing on the table at that time. Anything lower and you should consider folding. In stud poker, a playable hand is a minimum of a high pair (for example, two 8s).

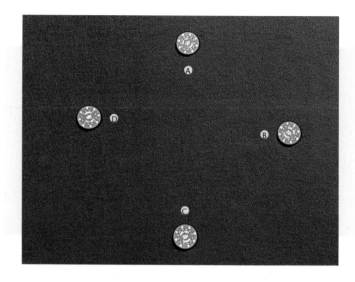

**1** PLAYERS BEGIN THE GAME BY SEEDING THE POT.

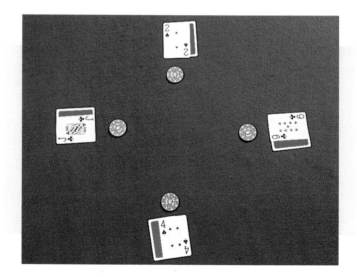

**2** TWO CARDS ARE DEALT TO EACH PLAYER, ONE FACE UP AND THE OTHER FACE DOWN. THE PLAYERS LOOK AT THEIR FACE-DOWN CARD.
PLAYER A HAS NOTHING OF VALUE.
PLAYER B HAS A PAIR OF 9s—AN INITIAL HAND WORTH PLAYING.
PLAYERS C AND D HAVE A JACK EACH, WHICH IS ALSO WORTH PLAYING.
PLAYER A'S DOWN CARD: 5♣   PLAYER B'S DOWN CARD: 9♠
PLAYER C'S DOWN CARD: J♦   PLAYER D'S DOWN CARD: 7♥

**3** PLAYER A MUST BET FIRST, AS HE IS SHOWING THE LOWEST FACE-UP CARD.

**4** TO STAY IN THE GAME, EACH PLAYER MAKES A BET EQUAL TO PLAYER A'S BET.

**5** THE NEXT ROUND OF CARDS IS DEALT.
PLAYER A'S NEW CARD:   8♦
PLAYER B'S NEW CARD:   A♦
PLAYER C'S NEW CARD:   4♦
PLAYER D'S NEW CARD:   7♣

**6** PLAYER B IS SHOWING THE HIGHEST RANKING HAND (WITH AN ACE AS THE HIGH CARD) AND MUST BET FIRST.
PLAYERS C AND D CALL (THEY MAKE A BET EQUAL TO PLAYER B'S BET).

**7** PLAYER A FOLDS. HIS CARDS ARE RETURNED TO THE DEALER, AND HE LOSES HIS STAKE.

**8** THE NEXT CARD IS DEALT.
PLAYER B'S NEW CARD: 4♥
PLAYER C'S NEW CARD: 3♥
PLAYER D'S NEW CARD: 3♣

**9** PLAYER C IS NOW SHOWING THE HIGHEST RANKING HAND WITH A PAIR OF 4s, SO BETS FIRST.

**10** PLAYER C RAISES. PLAYERS B AND D CALL. THE NEXT CARD IS THEN DEALT.
PLAYER B'S NEW CARD: A♣
PLAYER C'S NEW CARD: J♠
PLAYER D'S NEW CARD: 7♦

**11** PLAYER B HAS TWO PAIRS (ACES OVER 9S) AND KNOWS HE HAS BEATEN PLAYER C'S HAND UNLESS PLAYER C HAS THREE OF A KIND WITH FOURS. THE FACT THAT PLAYER B HAS A 4 IN HIS HAND MAKES IT LESS LIKELY THAT C HAS THREE OF A KIND.

PLAYER B CAN ALSO SEE THAT IF PLAYER D HAS TWO PAIRS, HE HAS BEATEN HIM. HOWEVER, HE KNOWS THAT IF PLAYER D HAS THREE OF A KIND WITH 7S, THEN PLAYER D WILL WIN.

PLAYER C HAS TWO PAIRS (JACKS OVER 4S). PLAYER C CAN SEE THAT B HAS A POSSIBLE TWO PAIRS, WHICH WOULD BEAT HIS TWO PAIRS, AND THAT D HAS A POSSIBLE THREE OF A KIND, WHICH WOULD ALSO BEAT HIS HAND.

PLAYER D HAS THREE OF A KIND WITH 7S. HE KNOWS THAT PLAYER B CAN ONLY BEAT HIM IF HIS HOLE (DOWN) CARD IS AN ACE. D KNOWS HE HAS BEATEN PLAYER C'S BEST POSSIBLE HAND OF THREE OF A KIND (WITH 4S).

AS PLAYER B IS SHOWING THE HIGHEST RANKING HAND, WITH A PAIR OF ACES, HE BETS FIRST.

**12** PLAYER B RAISES AGAIN.
PLAYER C REALIZES HE CANNOT MATCH THE OTHER PLAYERS AND FOLDS. HIS CARDS ARE REMOVED BY THE DEALER, AND HE LOSES HIS STAKE.

**13** PLAYER D MEETS PLAYER B'S CHALLENGE AND RAISES.
IN RESPONSE, PLAYER B RAISES AGAIN.

**14** PLAYER D RAISES.

(EACH RAISE BET MUST BE MET OR EXCEEDED BY THE NEXT PLAYER IF HE OR SHE WANTS TO REMAIN IN THE GAME.)

**15** PLAYER B CALLS (BETS THE SAME AMOUNT AS PLAYER D'S LAST BET).

**16** PLAYER D RAISES.

PLAYER B LOSES HIS NERVE AND IS NOW CONVINCED THAT PLAYER D MUST HAVE THREE OF A KIND, SO HE FOLDS.

**17** PLAYER D WINS THE POT.

PLAYER D HOLDS: 7♥ 7♣ 7♦ J♣ 3♣

HIS WINNING CARDS WERE THREE OF A KIND: 7♥ 7♣ 7♦

ABOVE *The fine art of the showdown is depicted in this 1895 lithograph. High-stakes poker games require nerves of steel, a cool head, and an inscrutable countenance if a player is to outwit his equally cunning opponents.*

# *Game Speak*

*All-in* – a player who runs out of funds, but may continue to play for his contribution to the pot

*Ante* – initial bet

*Babies* – low cards

*Blind bet* – a bet made before a hand is seen

*Bluff* – to pretend you have a good hand

*Bullet* – an ace

*Burned card* – a card discarded to combat cheating

*Button* – a marker denoting the player to bet first

*Call* – to bet the same as a previous bet

*Community cards* – cards laid face up on the table in Hold 'em and Omaha, and used by all players

*Dead man's hand* – two pairs (aces over 8s)

*Flop* – the first three community cards in Hold 'em or Omaha

*Fold* – to surrender from the game

*Forced bet* – the bet made to start the game

*Hole cards* – unseen cards in the player's hand

*Kicker* – the extra card retained in draw poker to make a hand appear better than it is

*Muck pile* – where the losing cards are placed

*Raise* – to make an increased bet

*Showdown* – when players reveal their cards

*Trips* – three of a kind

*Open* – to make the first bet

*Pot* – the total stakes that are played for

Each player receives a total of seven cards, and the aim is to make the best possible hand from those cards. Three cards are initially dealt (two face down and one face up). The player with the lowest up card makes a forced bet. A button (marker) then travels around the table to indicate which player is to make the forced bet in the next game.

After the forced bet, each player may fold, call, or raise when it is his or her turn. The fourth, fifth, and sixth cards are dealt face up and the seventh face down. After each card is dealt, there is a round of betting. The player with the highest ranking hand on view is the first to either bet or fold in each round of betting.

After all seven cards have been dealt, four cards are on display to the other players, and three are hidden from view. With each round of betting, players obtain more information on which to base their strategy, enabling a player to deduce what chance his or her cards have of winning.

If a player's visible cards have the potential to make a good hand, he or she has the option of bluffing, even if there is nothing of value in his or her hidden cards. By continually raising the stakes, it is possible to force the other players into folding—in which case the player's bluff will have been called, and he or she will win without having to reveal his or her own hand.

Because the players receive seven cards, there is a much better chance of making higher ranking hands, so the strategy in this game is entirely different from other forms of poker.

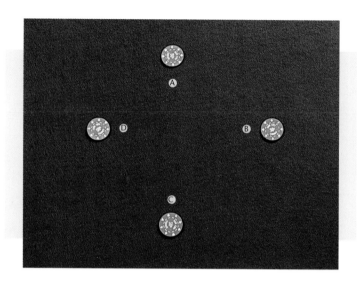

**1** THE AIM OF SEVEN-CARD STUD IS TO MAKE THE BEST POSSIBLE FIVE-CARD POKER HAND FROM THE SEVEN CARDS DEALT.
TO BEGIN PLAYING, THE POT IS SEEDED.

**2** EACH PLAYER RECEIVES THREE CARDS (TWO FACE DOWN AND ONE FACE UP). PLAYER C HAS THE LOWEST UP CARD, SO MAKES A FORCED BET.
PLAYER A DOWN: 10♥ 10♠    PLAYER B DOWN: Q♥ Q♦
PLAYER C DOWN: 10♦ 4♥    PLAYER D DOWN: 6♣ 6♦

**3** AFTER THE FORCED BET, EACH PLAYER IN TURN MAY FOLD, CALL, OR RAISE.
THE FOURTH, FIFTH, AND SIXTH CARDS ARE DEALT FACE UP, AND THE
SEVENTH IS DEALT FACE DOWN.
PLAYER A HAS A PAIR OF 10S IN HIS HOLE (DOWN) CARDS.
PLAYER B HAS A PAIR OF QUEENS IN HIS HOLE CARDS.
PLAYER C HAS NOTHING.
PLAYER D HAS A PAIR OF 6S.

**4** AFTER EACH CARD IS DEALT, THERE IS A ROUND OF BETTING.
THE PLAYER WITH THE HIGHEST CARD ON VIEW IS THE FIRST TO BET OR FOLD
IN EACH ROUND.
WHEN ALL THE CARDS HAVE BEEN DEALT, FOUR CARDS ARE ON DISPLAY, AND
THREE ARE HIDDEN FROM VIEW.

**5** PLAYERS A AND B BOTH HAVE TWO PAIRS (B'S PAIRS ARE HIGHER).
PLAYER C HAS A STRAIGHT.
PLAYER D HAS A FULL HOUSE.
ON A SHOWDOWN, PLAYER D'S HAND WINS.

IN THE FINAL OUTCOME, PLAYER D WON, BUT IN SEVEN-CARD STUD, OUT-
COMES ARE NOT ALWAYS PREDICTABLE.
PLAYER B HAD A GOOD INITIAL HAND AND SHOULD HAVE ATTEMPTED TO
FORCE THE OTHER PLAYERS INTO FOLDING BEFORE THEY IMPROVED ON
THEIR HANDS.
BY PUSHING THE BETTING HIGH EARLY ON, PLAYER D MIGHT HAVE BEEN
FORCED TO FOLD, AS INITIALLY HE ONLY HAD A LOW PAIR.
PLAYER C HAD NOTHING SPECIAL IN HIS HOLE CARDS AND COULD ALSO
HAVE BEEN FORCED OUT EARLY—BUT BY STAYING IN, HE IMPROVED TO A
GOOD HAND.

THE PLAYERS UP (VISIBLE) CARDS ARE:

| | | | | |
|---|---|---|---|---|
| PLAYER A UP: | J♦ | 4♦ | 2♦ | 4♠ |
| PLAYER B UP: | 9♦ | A♦ | A♠ | 2♥ |
| PLAYER C UP: | 5♦ | 3♠ | 5♥ | 6♥ |
| PLAYER D UP: | 9♦ | 6♠ | 8♥ | 3♦ |

THE PLAYERS DOWN (HIDDEN) CARDS ARE:

| | | | |
|---|---|---|---|
| PLAYER A DOWN: | 10♥ | 10♠ | 3♥ |
| PLAYER B DOWN: | Q♥ | Q♦ | K♠ |
| PLAYER C DOWN: | 10♦ | 4♥ | 7♣ |
| PLAYER D DOWN: | 6♣ | 6♦ | 8♦ |

Each player receives two cards face down. Five cards are placed face up in the center of the table. These cards are called community cards and are used by all the players. Each player uses a combination of the two cards in his or her hand and the five community cards to make the best possible five-card hand.

The game begins with the players being dealt their two hole (down) cards. After they look at them, a round of betting follows. The player to the left of the dealer makes an ante bet (called a small blind), and the player after him makes a second bet, normally double the value (called the big blind). The other players bet by matching at least the value of the big blind. This helps to increase the pot.

When the first round of betting is complete, three of the community cards are dealt face up (the flop). Another round of betting follows, with the players now assessing their chances of making a winning hand from the cards they hold, plus the revealed community cards. Players who feel that they have no cards of any value will fold at this stage.

After the next community card (the turn) is dealt, there is a further round of betting before the final community card (the river) is dealt, followed by more betting. The way in which players bet is an indication of their hands. The flop also gives an indication of what hands are possible. Before the flop, each player needs to decide whether or not his or her hand is worth playing. It is worth playing if the cards include any pair (not just a high pair), consecutive cards of the same suit, or fairly high cards of the same suit.

After the flop, the players have more information and can see what their possible hands might be. Occasionally, a player may be in a position where he or she knows that his or her hand is the best hand possible—called nuts. Whatever happens, the player can't lose. In this situation, the player needs to tread carefully, as increasing the stakes too quickly could result in other players dropping out too soon. The objective in these circumstances is to keep the other players betting for as long as possible, to keep increasing the pot.

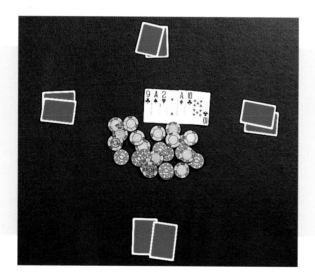

PLAYER A'S HOLE (HIDDEN) CARDS ARE TWO ACES. HE STAYS IN THE GAME.

PLAYER B HAS TWO LOW CARDS AND FOLDS.

PLAYER C HAS A PAIR OF 8S.

PLAYER D HAS A KING AND JACK OF THE SAME SUIT.

AFTER THE TURN, PLAYER A THINKS HE IS IN A POSITION TO HAVE THE BEST POSSIBLE HAND (NUTS).

ONCE ALL THE COMMUNITY CARDS HAVE BEEN DEALT, PLAYER A KNOWS HE HAS NUTS. HE NEEDS TO TRY TO KEEP THE BETTING GOING TO INCREASE THE POT, AS HE KNOWS HE CAN'T FAIL TO WIN.

Each player receives four cards face down (hole cards). Five community cards are placed face up in the center of the table, to be used by all the players. Players win by making the best possible ranking hand using two of the cards in their own hand, plus any three of the community cards. The game is dealt in a similar way to Hold 'em. Four cards are dealt, followed by the flop (the first three community cards). The remaining two community cards are dealt individually.

After each deal, there is a round of betting. Betting blind is also a possibility. After looking at their hole cards, players decide whether or not the hand is worth playing.

Unlike other versions of poker, conventional scoring is not always going to produce a winning hand. For example, four of a kind is not worth playing, as only two of the hole cards can be used, which gives a pair, and this cannot be improved upon.

Three of a kind is not a good hand either, as there is only a small chance of receiving the fourth in the community cards. The same is also true of being dealt four cards that might make a flush (five cards of the same suit in any numerical order), as the chances of a player making a flush from the community cards are drastically reduced.

In Omaha, the best cards to play with are a high pair or two high cards of the same suit, either of which could lead to a flush.

After the flop, a player needs to force out any other player who could potentially beat his or her hand. In Omaha it is also possible for a player to have nuts—the best possible hand.

PLAYER A HAS TWO HIGH CARDS OF THE SAME SUIT.

PLAYER B HAS A KING AND A 10.

PLAYER C HAS FOUR OF A KIND IN HIS HOLE CARDS.

AS HE HAS NO CHANCE OF IMPROVING, HE FOLDS.

PLAYER D HAS A PAIR OF QUEENS.

PLAYERS A, B, AND D MAKE THEIR BETS.

THE FLOP REVEALS THAT PLAYER A HAS A STRAIGHT.

HE KNOWS ONLY A HIGHER STRAIGHT CAN BEAT HIM.

B HAS A FULL HOUSE AND KNOWS ONLY A FLUSH CAN BEAT HIM.

PLAYER D DOES NOT IMPROVE, SO FOLDS.

BETTING CONTINUES BETWEEN PLAYERS A AND B.

IF NEITHER FOLDS, THE GAME WILL GO TO A SHOWDOWN, WHICH PLAYER A WILL WIN.

In Caribbean stud (or casino) poker, the players bet against the dealer instead of the other players. Up to seven players can play at one time. It is played on a special table and uses a single deck of 52 cards.

To enter the game, players make an initial bet by placing a chip in the box marked "ante." The dealer deals five cards face down to each player and five cards to himself (four face down and the fifth face up). After looking at their cards, the players decide whether to play or fold. If a player folds, the dealer takes the cards and the ante bet is lost.

If a player decides to play, another bet (the bonus bet) of twice the ante must be made and placed in the box marked "raise." Wins are paid at a predetermined bonus rate for this bet (see table below).

When all the players have placed their bets, the dealer reveals his down cards. To play, the dealer must hold at least one ace or king. If the dealer qualifies, each player's hand is compared with the dealer's. If a player has a higher hand, his or her ante bet is paid at odds of evens, and his or her raise (bonus) bet is paid according to the table of odds. If the player's hand ranks lower than the dealer's, both the ante and the raise bets are lost. If the dealer's hand does not qualify, the ante bet is paid at even money and the raise bet is returned.

### ODDS ON RAISE (BONUS) BET

| HAND | BONUS |
|---|---|
| Straight flush | 50 to 1 |
| Four of a kind | 20 to 1 |
| Full house | 7 to 1 |
| Flush | 6 to 1 |
| Straight | 4 to 1 |
| Three of a kind | 3 to 1 |
| Two pairs | 2 to 1 |
| One pair | even money |

1 PLAYERS A AND B EACH MAKE A BET OF ONE CHIP IN THE ANTE BOX.
PLAYER C MAKES A BET OF TWO CHIPS.
FIVE CARDS ARE DEALT TO EACH PLAYER AND FIVE TO THE DEALER.
THE DEALER'S LAST CARD IS DEALT FACE UP. IT IS A 5.
THE PLAYERS LOOK AT THEIR CARDS. PLAYER A HAS 2 PAIRS.
PLAYER B HAS NOTHING. PLAYER C HAS A FULL HOUSE.

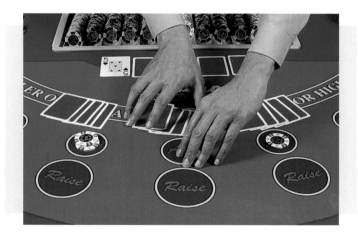

2 THE PLAYERS NOW HAVE TO DECIDE WHETHER TO PLAY OR SURRENDER.
PLAYER B SURRENDERS, AND HIS CARDS ARE REMOVED.
THE STAKE (ANTE) IS LOST AND IS REMOVED BY THE DEALER.

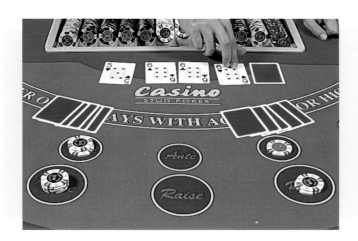

**3** PLAYER A MAKES A RAISE (BONUS) BET OF TWO CHIPS (DOUBLE THE VALUE OF THE ORIGINAL ANTE BET).
PLAYER C MAKES A RAISE BET OF FOUR CHIPS (DOUBLE THE ANTE BET OF TWO CHIPS).

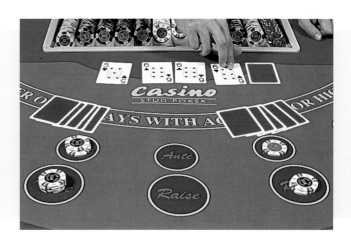

**4** THE DEALER'S CARDS ARE REVEALED.
THE DEALER HAS THREE OF A KIND.

**5** THE PLAYERS' HANDS ARE REVEALED IN TURN.
PLAYER A LOSES BOTH THE ANTE BET AND THE BONUS BET, AS THE DEALER'S THREE OF A KIND RANKS HIGHER THAN HIS TWO PAIRS.

**6** PLAYER C HAS A FULL HOUSE.
HE WINS AS HIS HAND RANKS HIGHER THAN THE DEALER'S.
THE ANTE BET IS PAID AT EVENS, AND THE BONUS BET IS PAID AT ODDS OF 7 TO 1.
PLAYER C HOLDS:  J♦ J♥ 5♠ 5♦ 5♣
DEALER HOLDS:   6♠ 6♦ 6♥ Q♠ 5♥

# BACCARA &

*The high stakes card game*

# BACCARAT

Baccara is the highest staking of all casino games. It originated in Italy during the Middle Ages, before migrating to France where it was popular with the aristocracy. It is the game played by James Bond and real-life legends, sometimes in public, but more often in the secluded confines of the *salon privé*. Baccara is particularly popular with high rollers, who often play games with no stake limit. It is not unusual for millions of dollars to be won or lost on the turn of a card. Nowadays, baccara is found in Europe's most exclusive casinos, such as Baden Baden and Monte Carlo.

Baccarat (with a silent "t"), also known as punto banco, is a simplified version of baccara which originated in the U.K. The name used depends on where the game is played. Punto banco is the British term, and baccarat tends to be used in the U.S.A.

RIGHT *Can you beat the bank? Only two hands are dealt in baccara, and players must beat the banker to win.*

LEFT *In the high-staking game of baccara, fortunes can be won or lost on the turn of a card.*

ABOVE *Up to 14 players can be seated at a full-size baccarat or punto banco table. In baccarat and punto banco the casino functions as the banker, so there is less risk to the players than in baccara, where the stakes are much higher.*

# THE EUROPEAN GAME

## BACCARA

Baccara, the forerunner of baccarat and punto banco, is played mostly in European casinos. It is particularly popular in both France and Germany. High minimum stakes are the norm in baccara, and it is not unusual to find games with a minimum stake of $100. Some games even start as high as $1000 minimum.

The large baccara tables, which can accommodate up to 14 players, are often located in a separate room in the casino, with entry to the highest staking games closed to all but the participants. The players and the casino dealer are seated around the table, but if there are more than 14 players, the others may stand. Each playing position is marked with a number.

Six decks of playing cards are used. Because of the size of the table, the dealer uses a large paddle to move the cards and chips around. The game is played with "community hands." No matter how many players there are, only two hands are dealt. One player, acting as the banker, receives one hand, and the remaining players bet on the other hand.

In most games, the house (the casino) acts as the banker and is responsible for paying out winnings and collecting losing bets. In baccara, however, the players take turns to act as the banker.

The player whose turn it is to be the banker stakes an amount of money that will be used to pay out all winning bets, which are paid at odds of evens. Losing bets are collected by the dealer and paid to the banker. The casino deducts a five percent commission from the losing bets. The banker is also responsible for dealing the cards. The ability to provide sufficient funds to cover all bets is what makes baccara a rich man's game.

The casino dealer's role is to control the game, pay out the winning bets from the banker's stake, collect the losing bets from the other players on the banker's behalf, and shuffle the cards. The casino dealer may also be consulted for advice. If a player consults the dealer, then the advice given must be followed.

## SCORING

Cards from two to nine inclusive have their face value. Aces count as one. Tens and the court cards (kings, queens, and jacks) all have a value of 0 (zero). Two cards are dealt to the player and two to the banker. The value of the cards is added together to give the score. If the score adds up to 10, the total becomes zero. If the total exceeds 10, then the score is the last digit, so a total of 14 becomes a score of four. The lowest possible score is zero, and the highest is nine. The winning hand is the one with the total closest to nine.

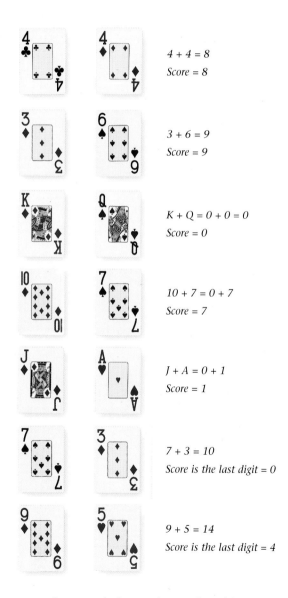

$4 + 4 = 8$
*Score = 8*

$3 + 6 = 9$
*Score = 9*

$K + Q = 0 + 0 = 0$
*Score = 0*

$10 + 7 = 0 + 7$
*Score = 7*

$J + A = 0 + 1$
*Score = 1*

$7 + 3 = 10$
*Score is the last digit = 0*

$9 + 5 = 14$
*Score is the last digit = 4*

**ABOVE** *Scores made from various card combinations.*

## PLAYING THE GAME

The object of baccara is to use a minimum of two and a maximum of three cards to try to make a score as close as possible to nine. The highest score is nine, and the lowest is zero. Players aim to win the money in the bank by beating the banker's hand.

After the dealer has shuffled the cards, a player is invited to cut them by placing a blank card into the pack. A second blank card is inserted about 15 cards from the end before the cards are placed in the shoe (sabot) and passed to the player acting as the banker, who deals. When the blank card is reached, the shoe is returned to the dealer for the cards to be reshuffled.

To begin a game, the banker makes an initial bet, called the bank (*banque* or *banco*). This bet can be any amount over the minimum table limit, and there is no upper limit to the amount that may be bet. Chips representing the bank are placed in front of the dealer.

TOP *Before the cards are placed in the shoe, a card is dealt face up, and cards equal to that number are discarded. If the card is an 8, eight cards are discarded.*

RIGHT *Certain scores result in specific actions. If a natural is dealt, the cards are immediately revealed. A baccara requires that a third card is drawn.*

The other players (the ponte or punto) may place bets against the bank up to its total amount. Players call out what they want to bet. If a player wants to bet an amount equal to the bank, he or she calls *"banco solo."* If more than one player calls *"banco solo,"* the player closest to the banker's right has precedence (seated players take precedence over standing players). The player sitting to the immediate right of the banker is known as the prime right.

A call of *"banco avec la table"* is a bet of half the bank's total, and other players may only bet up to the balance of the bank. A player who loses after playing either *banco solo* or *banco avec la table* takes precedence over prime right on the next hand *(banco suivi)*.

Once all the bets have been placed, the banker (banco) deals four cards face down. The player (ponte) with the highest stake receives the first and third card. The banker receives the second and fourth card.

After looking at the cards, the ponte makes certain plays depending on the score. With a score of zero to four, a third card is drawn (it will be dealt face up). With a score of five, taking a third card is optional.

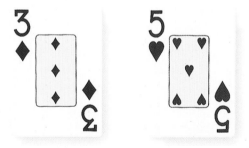

*A score of eight or nine is called a natural.*

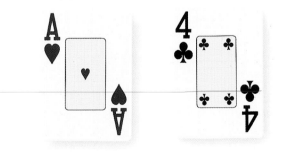

*Baccara is a score between zero and five.*

With six or seven, no action is taken and the player stands. A score of eight or nine (called a natural) is immediately revealed (turned face up). Any score between zero and five is called baccara.

If the player (ponte) has a score of eight or nine, the banker cannot take a third card, regardless of his score and he must stand (see table opposite)—but for any other total, the player must follow the rules for drawing a third card, according to the table below.

ACTION TO BE FOLLOWED BY THE PLAYER AFTER THE<br>FIRST TWO CARDS ARE DEALT

| Total score | Action to be taken |
| --- | --- |
| 0, 1, 2, 3, 4 | A third card is drawn |
| 5 | Taking a third card is optional |
| 6, 7 | No action is taken |
| 8, 9 | Hand is immediately revealed |

The banker's decision about whether or not to take a third card depends on the player's action. If the banker does not have a total of eight or nine, then the same action as the player is taken.

If the banker has a score of five, a third card **must** be drawn. If the player has drawn a third card, then the banker's decision depends on his score and the value of the player's third card.

If the ponte mistakenly draws a card when the rules say he should stand, the value is added to his hand, which can result in a winning hand losing.

In some casinos, neither the banker, nor a player who has bet an equal amount *(banco solo),* is obliged to follow the rules about drawing cards and has more freedom to choose his or her course of action.

A player who accepts the bank must pay its full value. If no player accepts the bank, it is offered to the highest bidder.

RIGHT *When the banker wins in baccara, five percent commission is deducted from the losing bets before the balance is paid to the banker. In baccarat or punto banco, the commission and losing bets are paid to the casino.*

ACTION TO BE FOLLOWED BY THE BANKER AFTER<br>THE PLAYER DRAWS A THIRD CARD

| Banker's score | Player's third card | Banker's action |
| --- | --- | --- |
| 3 | 8 | stands |
| 3 | Anything other than 8 | draws |
| 4 | 2, 3, 4, 5, 6, 7 | draws |
| 4 | 0, 1, 8, 9 | stands |
| 5 | 0, 1, 2, 3, 8, 9 | stands |
| 5 | 4, 5, 6, 7 | draws |
| 6 | 0, 1, 2, 3, 4 ,5, 8, 9 | stands |
| 6 | 6, 7 | draws |
| 7 | 0, 1, 2, 3, 4, 5, 8, 9 | stands |
| 8, 9 | Player cannot draw | stands |

The winner is the player with the highest score up to nine. If the ponte's score ties with the banker's, the hand is replayed. When the ponte wins, the bets are paid out from the bank at evens. When the banker wins, the dealer collects the losing bets from the pontes, deducts five percent commission, and adds the remainder to the bank.

If the banker wins, he or she may choose to keep the bank or pass it to the right. If the banker loses, the bank automatically passes to the right, but players are not obliged to accept it. It is worth keeping the bank if you have it, as the house advantage (or house edge—the percentage of the stake retained by the casino as profit) for the bank is lower, at 1.17 percent, than the house edge for the players, which is 1.23 percent.

# THE MODERN ARISTOCRATS

## BACCARAT & PUNTO BANCO

These are played on smaller tables and are dealt at a faster speed than baccara. Minimum stakes are around $5, which is considerably less than the high stakes normally played for at traditional baccara tables.

Baccarat and punto banco differ from baccara in that the casino acts as the banker, paying out winnings and collecting losing bets. In American casinos, baccarat players take turns to act as the dealer, but in punto banco, that role is fulfilled by the casino.

Between four and eight decks of cards are used, and the game is still played with community cards (all the players bet on the same hand). The rules on scoring and drawing cards are the same as for baccara.

Players have three choices when betting. They can bet on the banker (the casino), on the player, or on a tie between the two. The odds paid for a tie vary, but are normally 8 to 1. It is not worth betting on a tie, as the high house advantage makes it poor value.

To begin the game, the dealer shuffles the cards and invites a player to cut them by placing a blank card into the pack. The dealer places the cards in the shoe (sabot) and inserts a blank card about one deck from the end to indicate when the cards will be reshuffled. After each player has made his or her bet, four cards are dealt face down by the dealer. The cards for the player's hand are placed in the area of the table marked "Punto" or "Player." The player looks at the cards and draws additional cards according to the rules (refer to the tables on the previous page).

When the player's score is determined, the banker's hand is dealt with according to the rules. In the case of a tie, neither the bets on the player (punto) nor the banker (banco) lose, and bets on the tie are paid out. Winning bets on the player are paid at evens. Winning bets on the banker are also paid at evens, less five percent commission, which works out at odds of 19 to 20.

Baccarat is the big money game in U.S. casinos. Millions of dollars can be won or lost in a few minutes, and a casino's profit or loss statement can be directly affected by one player's foray at the baccarat tables.

RIGHT *In the 1965 movie* Thunderball, *Sean Connery, as James Bond, is inscrutable as he ponders a critical decision at the baccarat table.*

BELOW *Mini and midi punto banco tables are about the size of blackjack tables. The rules are the same, but the game is played much faster.*

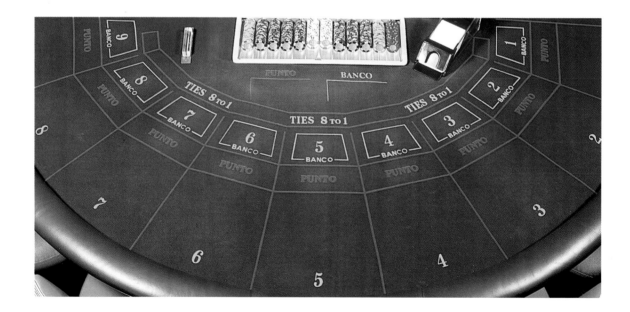

# Game Speak

*Baccara* – any score between zero and five

*Banco* – the player representing the bank

*Banco solo* – a player making a bet equal to the entire value of the bank

*Banque* – the bank

*Cagnotte* – commission

*Egalité* – a tie

*Natural* – a score of eight or nine

*Ponte* – a player

*Prime right* – the player sitting immediately to the right of the banker

*Punto* – a player

*Sabot* or *shoe* – the box in which cards are placed for dealing after they have been shuffled

**1** MOST CASINOS OFFER PUNTO BANCO ON MINI OR MIDI TABLES, AS THE GAMES ARE SIMPLER TO OPERATE AND EASIER TO PLAY. THE DIFFERENCE BETWEEN THEM IS THE NUMBER OF PLAYERS THEY CAN ACCOMMODATE.

**2** THE GAME BEGINS WITH THE PLAYERS MAKING THEIR BETS. PLAYER A (ON THE LEFT) BETS FIVE CHIPS ON PLAYER (PUNTO). PLAYER B BETS FIVE CHIPS ON BANKER (BANCO). PLAYER C BETS FIVE CHIPS ON A TIE.

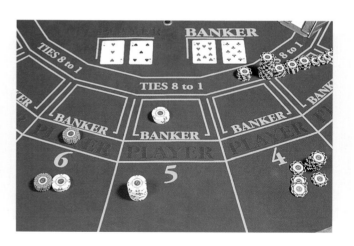

**3** TWO CARDS ARE DEALT FACE UP TO EACH HAND. THE PLAYER (PONTE) IS DEALT 5 AND 3, WHICH IS A SCORE OF EIGHT. THE BANK (BANCO) IS DEALT 10 AND 8. AS 10 COUNTS FOR 0 (ZERO), THIS IS ALSO A SCORE OF EIGHT, WHICH MEANS THERE IS A TIE.

**4** PLAYER C'S BET ON A TIE IS PAID OUT AT 8 TO 1. THE CARDS ARE CLEARED AWAY, AND THE GAME CONTINUES.

**5** PLAYER A BETS ON THE PLAYER AGAIN, AND PLAYER B ON THE BANKER.
PLAYER C DOES NOT BET THIS TIME.
TWO NEW HANDS ARE DEALT.
THE PONTE RECEIVES 9 AND 4—A SCORE OF THREE $(9 + 4 = 13 = 3)$
WHICH MEANS A THIRD CARD MUST BE DRAWN.

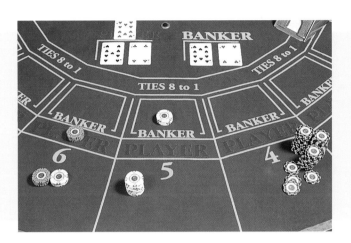

**6** ANOTHER CARD IS DEALT TO THE PLAYER. IT IS A 10 AND, AS THIS COUNTS
AS ZERO, THE SCORE REMAINS THREE.
THE BANKER RECEIVED $4 + 10$ WHICH TOTALS FOUR $(0 + 4 = 4)$.
THE BANKER HAS THE HIGHEST SCORE UP TO NINE, SO WINS THE HAND.

**7** THE BANKER WINS, AND THE BET IS PAID AT EVENS.

**8** THE PLAYER'S BET LOSES, AND THE STAKE IS REMOVED.

# CASINOS OF THE WORLD

*Money talks, whatever the language*

MANY casinos form part of hotel and leisure complexes located in tourist destinations, such as Sun City in South Africa and Atlantis in the Bahamas. However, there is nowhere else that embraces the gambling culture quite like Las Vegas. Over the years, it has grown from a desert oasis into an international resort and vacation destination, offering round-the-clock gaming and high quality entertainment in outstanding, if sometimes unusual, surroundings. Tourists visit to marvel at the amazing architecture that has become a trademark of the city, bringing elements of Paris, Rome, Venice, and Egypt together in one place. By contrast, most European casinos seem small and demure, offering no-frills gaming. City-center casinos in Europe cater largely to tourists, while provincial casinos attract mostly local clientele.

RIGHT *At Treasure Island, in Las Vegas, a pirate show, which takes place every 90 minutes, culminates in the sinking of the* HMS Britannia.

LEFT *Atlantis Casino Resort, on Paradise Island in the Bahamas, recreates the legend of the ancient city that vanished beneath the waves*

# UNITED STATES

## LAS VEGAS

Gambling was legalized in Nevada on March 19, 1931, but in the early days, Las Vegas was very much under the control of the Mob. However, during the 1960s, a number of major corporations began running the casinos, transforming them into legitimate businesses. The 1980s were a time of major growth and investment, with new casinos being built on a grand scale.

Nowadays, the casinos of Las Vegas are huge entertainment complexes. The most lavish and expensive are found around The Strip, otherwise known as Las Vegas Boulevard, the street that forms the heart of the city. They compete to offer the most spectacular shows and attractions, which feature such anachronisms as replicas of ancient Egypt and Rome, a medieval castle, the Manhattan skyline, and a tropical rainforest. Many of the casinos are family friendly, with children's entertainment and amusement parks. New casinos continue to be built and renovated, with recent trends moving toward elegant European themes.

Much of early Las Vegas has disappeared, to be replaced by more recent developments. However, the Flamingo, the original casino that inspired the transformation of Las Vegas from a desert oasis into a gambling center, still exists. The area around Fremont Street, formerly known as Glitter Gulch, has been pedestrianized and covered with a canopy of over two million lights, creating a light and sound show called Sky Parade. The casinos here are less expensive than those on The Strip.

Las Vegas is one of the world's top entertainment centers. From the early days it has played host to stars including Frank Sinatra, Elvis Presley, Liza Minnelli, and more recently, Siegfried and Roy's Magic Show. The city is also a popular wedding venue.

LEFT *At night, The Strip blazes with color, as neon lights up the desert skies of Las Vegas, and rich and poor alike come out to stake their claim to a slice of the gambling cake, all hoping to hit the "big time."*

## BINION'S HORSESHOE

Situated in the Horseshoe Hotel on Fremont Street in downtown Las Vegas, Binion's gives a taste of how gambling used to be in the Old West. Opened in 1951 by Benny Binion, a former Texas bootlegger and gambler, the casino evokes the atmosphere of a traditional gambling hall—no shows, no music, just gambling. Minimum stakes are $2 on blackjack and $1 on craps. The poker tables are not for beginners, though, as many professional players make their living here.

The World Series of Poker has been held at Binion's since 1970. The first competition had seven players, but now over 650 players from around the world try their luck. Each May, Becky Binion opens the tournament with a call of "shuffle up 'n deal." The action takes place nonstop for 30 days, with a variety of tournaments offering stakes from $1 to no limit. The final is the No Limit Texas Hold 'em Tournament, which lasts four days. Players pay a $10,000 entrance fee and compete for the $1.5 million first prize and the title of world champion. The winner is given celebrity status, gaining a place in the Poker Hall of Fame.

Many players attempt to win their entrance fee by competing in satellite tournaments. Ten players each stake $1000 and play a knockout tournament, with the winner taking all the stakes. There are also super-satellites, where players each stake $100 and attempt to win the entry fee from a field of 200 or 300 gamblers.

The World Series of Poker was inspired by a poker marathon which took place in 1949 at Binion's Horseshoe between Nicolas "Nick the Greek" Dandolos and Johnny Moss. They played poker nonstop for five months, only taking breaks to sleep. Moss won and in 1970 repeated his success by becoming the winner of the first World Championship.

LEFT *Binion's Horseshoe aims to give players a better deal than its competitors. Low stakes and better payout odds make it the casino to visit for great value.*

RIGHT *Each night the lake outside Bellagio comes alive when 1000 fountains, reaching 240ft (73m) into the air, "dance" to a spectacular music and light show.*

## BELLAGIO

When Steve Wynn's Mirage Resorts opened Bellagio in 1998, no expense was spared to create one of the most elegant and luxurious hotels in Las Vegas.

Bellagio is a stylish recreation of its namesake, a scenic village overlooking Lake Como in northern Italy. The effect is accomplished with a 9 acre (3.6ha) man-made lake, lavish gardens, and terracotta tiled roofs on the buildings.

A boulevard leads past the lake to the hotel entrance, where a botanical garden is housed under a huge dome. Lush green foliage and brightly colored flowers surround classical-style columns. The garden is continually changed to complement the seasons.

High class restaurants offer diners a choice of award-winning French and Tuscan cuisine. The hotel's 3000 rooms are decorated with antiques and art. Facilities include a swimming pool, spa, and a shopping arcade featuring names such as Prada, Chanel, and Hermès. A monorail links Bellagio to the Monte Carlo next door.

The 110,000 sq ft (10,000m²) casino offers roulette, blackjack, craps, let it ride, pai gow, Caribbean stud poker, and baccarat. The table minimum starts at $5, rising to $10 at peak times.

# BALLYS

Hollywood movie stars Cary Grant and Raquel Welch performed the opening ceremony when Ballys was built in 1973, at a cost of $100 million.

In 1981, a second tower was added, and the hotel was expanded to over 2800 rooms. Now owned and operated by Park Place Entertainment, the Art Deco interior recently had a $72 million restoration. The complex includes restaurants and a shopping arcade.

Ballys is host to *Jubilee!,* Las Vegas' longest-running topless revue, with a cast of 100 dancers and singers, which opened in 1981 at a cost of $10 million. It was recently updated with a new $3 million opening number. The program of original song and dance acts includes reenactments of the sinking of the *Titanic,* and the destruction of the Temple of Samson.

The gaming floor covers 67,000 sq ft (6224m$^2$) with over 100 table games, including blackjack, roulette, baccarat, craps, poker, big six wheel, pai gow, and a new race and sports book with 11 jumbo screens and 210 personal monitors.

BELOW *Moving sidewalks featuring special effects give easy access from The Strip, and a monorail connects Ballys to the nearby MGM Grand.*

# CAESARS PALACE

First opened in 1966, Caesars Palace underwent a $300 million renovation in 1997. Many of the 2400 rooms feature spas, saunas, and Roman tubs. Adjacent to the hotel is the Forum, an ancient Roman streetscape with shops, boutiques, and restaurants, as well as a thrilling simulator ride, *Race for Atlantis.* The casino's Roman theme is also realized in the handpainted murals and classical sculptures that line the gaming rooms.

With three 24-hour casinos, Caesars offers some of the best gaming facilities in Las Vegas. Games available include roulette, craps, baccarat, big six, and Caribbean stud poker. Stakes start at $5 and increase when the casino is busy. A unique form of stud poker is played here, based on five-card stud. Blackjack games are available in many forms including hand-dealt single, double, and multiple deck games; games dealt from a shoe; and over/under 13 games. Stakes on the slot machines start from 5 cents. The venue, which has hosted many championship boxing tournaments, also offers a huge sports book.

BELOW *At Caesars Palace, monumental statues in marble and bronze recapture the golden age of Rome. A daily royal procession takes place in the Forum.*

# CIRCUS CIRCUS

Circus Circus comprises three casinos, plus a separate keno area. The main casino has over 1800 slots with a range of progressive games. Table games include roulette, blackjack, craps, poker, casino war, pai gow poker, and Caribbean stud poker. Stakes start at $3 for blackjack, $2 for craps, and $1 for roulette. The poker room has 10 tables featuring low limit games.

The West Casino has over 500 slots, plus roulette and blackjack tables. The SkyRise casino has over 400 slots, blackjack, and roulette. The race and sports book allows players the opportunity to gamble on horse or greyhound racing, and other sports events.

Family entertainment includes the world's largest permanent circus, the dramatic *Mystère Cirque du Soleil*. The cast of 72 acrobats, gymnasts, and dancers dazzle visitors with their polished routines and flying trapeze shows. The Adventure Dome theme park features the spectacular Canyon Blaster roller coaster and three motion-simulator rides. Couples can tie the knot at the Chapel of the Fountain.

BELOW *The Canyon Blaster, a double-loop double-corkscrew roller coaster, reaches 55 miles (85km) per hour as it swoops through the Adventure Dome.*

# EXCALIBUR

Located in one of the world's largest hotels, with 4008 rooms, the casino at Excalibur has 75 gaming tables offering blackjack, roulette, craps, and mini-baccarat, with stakes from $3–$5. Eleven poker tables offer a choice of seven-card stud, pai gow, Caribbean stud, Texas hold 'em, jackpot poker, and progressive poker.

There is also a 132-seat keno lounge and facilities to play keno in the restaurants. The race and sports book has 150 seats. The more than 2550 slots, which include electronic games, video poker, and video keno, offer stakes ranging from 5 cents to $25. The casino also has big six wheel, Spanish 21, and let it ride.

The medieval theme is embodied in King Arthur's Arena, where a nightly medieval jousting show, *The Tournament of Kings,* features battles between invading armies, brave knights, wizards, and a fire-breathing dragon. Other nongaming attractions include the Grand Slam Canyon—an in-house roller coaster, swimming pools with waterfalls and water slides, and a medieval shopping village.

BELOW *The battlements, turrets, and moat of the castle-like Excalibur Casino were inspired by the myths and legends of King Arthur's Round Table.*

## LAS VEGAS HILTON

The Las Vegas Hilton appeals to business people due to its excellent convention facilities. The gaming floor is spread over 67,000 sq ft (6224m²). It is dominated by the world's largest race and sports book, where a video wall made up of 46 screens, some of which are 15ft (4.5m) across, covers an area of 30,500 sq ft (2833m²). This is complemented by a state-of-the-art audio system. Games include slots, blackjack, craps, poker, keno, and roulette. Minimum stakes start at $5 and increase at peak times. There is also a large luxurious baccarat room, with crystal chandeliers and plush furniture.

Additional facilities include the 1600-seat Hilton Las Vegas Theater; a nightclub; 12 restuarants offering everything from burgers and fries to Japanese hibachi; and an 18-hole golf course. Another attraction is Star Trek—The Experience, an interactive museum housing a collection of props and costumes from the popular television show. Visitors are taken on a simulated journey through the Star Trek universe.

## LUXOR

A vast 30-story pyramid encloses the world's largest atrium, measuring 29 million cu ft (820,000m³). From its summit, the world's brightest beam of light reaches 10 miles (16km) into space. Attractions include the Ra nightclub; *Lasting Impressions*—a show starring Bill Acosta; a replica of Tutankhamen's tomb, discovered by Howard Carter in 1922; Luxor Live, a simulated talk show with hologram characters; and an Imax cinema.

The gaming area fills 120,000 sq ft (11,000m²) and features a race and sports book. Minimum table stakes start at $5, increasing to $10 on busy nights. Novice players can participate in poker lessons and try their luck in beginner's games with $1–$2 minimum stakes.

## MGM GRAND

Dubbed the "City of Entertainment," the MGM Grand promises "more facilities and recreational venues than any other resort." The Grand Garden Arena features world-class concerts and special events; EFX Theatre is home to a $45 million musical starring Tommy Tune; Hollywood Theater features top entertainers; and New York's famous Studio 54 nightclub is recreated. The MGM Lion Habitat showcases five lions—descendants of the company's famous mascot.

The Entertainment Dome houses the 170,000 sq ft (16,000m²) gaming area, where 165 tables offer craps, roulette, baccarat, mini-baccarat, Caribbean stud poker, pai gow, big six, Spanish 21, and keno. Stakes start at $5 and increase at busy times. There are 3700 slots with stakes from a 5 cents to $500. Tables in the race and sports book have their own TV sets and laptop points. The casino also has a sumptuous European-style area for high rollers.

LEFT *Recalling the golden era of Hollywood, the lavish MGM Grand incorporates 16 restaurants, the Showbar Lounge, and the Forever Grand Wedding Chapel.*

RIGHT *A replica of the Sphinx stands guard over the world's fourth largest pyramid. The interior walls are slanted, and the escalators move at a 39° angle.*

## THE MIRAGE

At dusk, the volcano outside The Mirage springs into life. Every 15 minutes, it erupts, spewing flames and smoke 100ft (30m) into the air and lava down its side.

The illusion continues inside Kokomo's Restaurant, where diners are surrounded by a tropical rainforest housed beneath a huge dome. Bathed in a fine mist of water, over 100 species of plants including orchids, bromeliads, and bird of paradise trees inhabit the unique indoor environment. Dolphin pools, an aquarium with live sharks, and a lagoon-style pool add to the paradise theme. The long-running show by world-famous illusionists Siegfried and Roy features the Royal White Tigers and the White Lions of Timbavati.

The casino has 117 table games and 2200 slot and video poker machines. Minimum stakes are 5 cents on slots and $5 on tables, rising to $25 at peak times.

Steve Wynn, the former head of Mirage Resorts, has helped transform Las Vegas into a sophisticated destination. When The Mirage opened in 1989 it set new standards in the city, which Wynn surpassed when he opened Bellagio in 1998, realizing his dream to create the "most romantic and exciting hotel in the world."

## NEW YORK NEW YORK

This casino take its theme from the "city that never sleeps," recreating the Manhattan skyline at one-third scale. Times Square, the Empire State building, the Chrysler building, and the public library provide a backdrop for a 150ft (45m) replica of the Statue of Liberty with a tugboat at its base. The Brooklyn Bridge links The Strip with Greenwich Village.

Cobbled streets are lined with tenement buildings, complete with graffiti. The Manhattan Express Roller Coaster, which reaches speeds of 67 mph (107 kph), runs across the skyline and into the casino, introducing a flavor of New York's Coney Island beach resort.

The interior of the 84,000 sq ft (7800m²) casino echoes New York's Central Park, with trees, streams, and bridges surrounding 74 gaming tables, 2000 slots, and a sports book. Games include roulette, blackjack, craps, mini-baccarat, progressive pai gow poker, Caribbean stud poker, let it ride, big six, casino war, and keno. Minimum stakes range from $5–$10.

## TREASURE ISLAND

Treasure Island, owned by Mirage Resorts, has a pirate theme. A free show takes place each evening outside the casino in Buccaneer Bay, where swashbuckling pirates from *Hispaniola* do battle with British naval officers from *HMS Britannia*. The exchange of canon and musket fire culminates in the sinking of the British vessel. Large crowds gather to watch, so it is best to arrive early to get a good vantage point.

Other amenities are the Mutiny Bay Entertainment Center; Pirate's Walk Shopping Promenade; a tropical pool area, spa and beauty salon; and a children's zoo. The Treasure Island casino is open 24 hours a day

LEFT *Among the attractions at The Mirage are white tigers, part of the casino's attempts to provide an environment with something for the whole family.*

RIGHT *The "Big Apple" comes to Las Vegas, in the form of the Manhattan skyline, complete with the Statue of Liberty and Coney Island roller coaster.*

# THE VENETIAN

Located at the heart of The Strip, The Venetian, which opened in 1999 at a cost of $2 billion, is built on the site of the legendary Sands Hotel. It is modeled on famous landmarks of Venice, including the Campanile tower, Doge's Palace, and the Rialto Bridge. Gondolas on the Grand Canal and masked carnival performers in St. Mark's Square add to the effect. The all-suite hotel has a 5 acre (2ha) pool deck surrounded by gardens. Attractions include Madame Tussaud's Celebrity Encounter, featuring famous Las Vegas icons such as Elvis Presley, Tom Jones, and Frank Sinatra.

The rococo-style casino has 122 gaming tables, offering blackjack, craps, roulette, pai gow, Caribbean stud poker, and let it ride. The minimum stake is $5, increasing at peak times. There is a race and sports book and keno lounge. There are 2500 slot machines with stakes ranging from 5 cents to $500.

# PARIS LAS VEGAS

Opened in 1999, the $760 million resort, owned by Park Place Entertainment, recreates the atmosphere of Paris, with replicas of Parisian landmarks including the Arc de Triomphe, the Louvre, and the Paris Opera House. The half-scale Eiffel Tower has glass lifts to the summit, from which point there is a panoramic view of Las Vegas.

The 83,000 sq ft (7900m²) casino, with 100 tables and 2200 slots, is a Parisian street scene, with cobblestone paths, wrought-iron streetlamps, and the ceiling painted to give the effect of the Paris sky at twilight. Games include blackjack, craps, roulette, Caribbean stud poker, and pai gow. Stakes start at $5, rising to $10 at peak times. The race and sports book provides live coverage of major events from around the world.

LEFT *The Doge's Palace is mirrored in the Grand Canal, and a gondola waits for passengers. One can almost hear the cry—Benvenuto a Venezia!*

RIGHT *Explore the sights of Paris without the language problem. Only in Las Vegas can visitors do a mini world tour in the space of a few hours.*

The decor in the 2916-room hotel is in the style of the historic Hotel de Ville in Paris. The roof has a 2 acre (1ha) swimming area set in a formal French garden. Passages in the convention area are inspired by the Hall of Mirrors at the Palace of Versailles.

Paris Las Vegas is linked to Ballys via Le Boulevard, a shopping mall with French-themed restaurants, and exclusive boutiques featuring some of Europe's top fashion names. Other facilities include a theater, European-style spa, and two wedding chapels.

# OTHER U.S. CASINOS

## MOHEGAN SUN

When expansions are completed in 2002, Mohegan
Sun, in Uncasville, Connecticut, is set to be one of the
the largest casino complexes in the world. Opened in
1996 by the Mohegan Tribal Nation, the expansion
will add a 1200-room luxury hotel, 10,000-seat arena,
new retail outlets, convention facilities that include
the Northeast's largest ballroom, and a second casino.

Decor throughout the complex draws on Mohegan
legend and tribal lore. The original Casino of the Earth
is a circular room divided into four sections, representing the four seasons of nature. The 179,500 sq ft
(16,700m²) gaming area has 3000 slot machines and
192 table games including high-stakes bingo, blackjack, craps, roulette, baccarat, and a separate poker
room. There is also a race book.

The new 115,000 sq ft (10,600m²) Casino of the Sky
will feature the world's largest planetarium dome, and
a multilevel onyx and alabaster venue, Wombi Rock,
housing a lounge and dance floor. Both casinos offer
nonsmoking gaming areas.

## BEAU RIVAGE

Beau Rivage, meaning beautiful shore, is situated in
the Gulf coast town of Biloxi, Mississippi. A feature of
Mississippi casinos is that they are required to float, so
the 72,000 sq ft (6700m²) casino has been built on a
barge. The 24-hour casino offers table games, slot
machines, a race book, and a separate poker room.

The Mediterranean-themed resort, built at a cost of
$675 million, opened in 1999. Mature oak trees line
the circular entrance which leads to an atrium planted
with flowers and fragrant magnolia trees. Finches fly
overhead, and the floor is an Italian-designed mosaic.

RIGHT *Mohegan Sun's new retail space is revealed in a*
*computer rendition. Symbolic "trees of life" line the*
*walkways, and "memory piles," resembling tradition-*
*al stone markers, house interactive shopping guides.*

# CARIBBEAN

## ATLANTIS

Located near Nassau in the Bahamas, the $850 million Atlantis resort on Paradise Island was opened by Sun International in 1998. The 826 acre (370ha) resort, surrounded by white beaches and crystal-clear water, is the perfect place to recreate the myth of Atlantis, the beautiful island that was overwhelmed by the sea.

The ruins of Atlantis are depicted in The Dig, an underwater labyrinth of walk-through tunnels which wind through 11 lagoons filled with over 200 species of marine life. Giant rays, barracuda, and sharks swim among fanciful relics of the ancient culture, including submarines and flying machines.

A life-size replica of a Mayan temple features water slides, such as the Serpent, which spins its riders into darkness to emerge in a clear tunnel that passes through the Predator Lagoon. The Jungle Slide meanders through exotic jungles, temples, and caves.

The resort's 2300 rooms are housed in four hotels. Included in the 176 suites is the 5,000 sq ft (465m²) Bridge Suite that spans the twin Royal Towers. The resort has 38 restaurants and bars offering a choice of Pacific Rim, American, and Italian cuisine.

The Entertainment Center, which houses the Caribbean's largest casino, has the unusual feature of opening onto outdoor terraces and restaurants, bringing the tropical environment of the Bahamas into the gaming area. The 78 gaming tables include roulette, blackjack, craps, baccarat, and Caribbean stud poker, as well as a high limit table area, the Baccarat Lounge. Stakes on the 980 slot machines range from 25 cents to $100. Free gaming lessons are offered daily.

LEFT *The Leap of Faith, a waterslide with an almost vertical 60ft (18m) drop, runs down the side of the Mayan temple and through a shark-filled lagoon.*

RIGHT *The Great Hall of Waters lobby at the 1200-room Royal Towers Hotel on Atlantis Paradise Island, the world's largest island resort destination.*

# EUROPE

In contrast to the huge resort casinos found in other parts of the world, European casinos are smaller, more tranquil establishments. Most are solely concerned with gaming and not with providing lavish Las Vegas-style accommodation and entertainment.

## MONTE CARLO

After gaming was introduced to Monaco (an enclave in France, near the Italian border) in 1857 by Prince Charles III, the Mediterranean principality flourished, becoming a playground for Europe's aristocracy, and a name synonymous with glamour and wealth.

Monte Carlo Casino, one of Europe's oldest, dates from 1863 and was designed by Charles Garnier, architect of the Paris Opera House. The classical buildings are set in formal gardens on a terrace overlooking the sea. There are several restaurants, including Les Privés, which has a sea view, and the Cabaret, which offers live shows. The Train Bleu restaurant recreates a deluxe dining car of a train from the *belle époque* era.

The sumptuously decorated gaming rooms feature marble columns, gilded mahogany, and chandeliers fashioned from Bohemian crystal. Games include blackjack, baccarat, French and American roulette, punto banco, craps, and *trente et quarante*.

Stakes start at 20 French francs for roulette, FF200 for blackjack, and FF500 for baccarat, chemin de fer and punto banco. There are 280 slot machines with stakes starting from F1. The casino is open daily from 12 p.m. to late. The minimum age for gambling is 21 years. Dress is smart, and men must wear ties.

The revamped Monte Carlo Sporting Club houses the futuristic Les Palmiers gaming hall, Maona restaurant, and Jimmy'z disco. Le Café de Paris, adjacent to the main casino, offers poker, craps, blackjack, and roulette, as well as bars, restaurants, and cabaret shows.

RIGHT *The classical facade of Monte Carlo Casino evokes an age when an evening at the gaming tables meant formal dress and an air of elegance.*

## BADEN BADEN

Germany's Baden Baden, famously described by Marlene Dietrich as the "most beautiful casino in the world", is also one of the oldest still in operation. It was opened in 1748 by Edouard Benazet, who employed Parisian craftsmen to design the stylish rooms that are now a tourist attraction in their own right.

The main gaming area, which totals over 32,000 sq ft (3000m²), comprises several luxuriously decorated rooms, including the Red Chamber, Austrian room, the Winter Garden, le Salon Madame de Pompadour, the Margrave Room, and the Florentine room.

The casino is open daily from 2 p.m. to late. Games include American roulette, baccarat, blackjack, poker, and slot machines. French rules apply. Minimum table limits are 5 deutsche marks for roulette and slots, DM10 for blackjack and poker, and DM100 for baccarat. The slot machines are housed in a separate building that was formerly the town's railway station.

Players must be over 21, and passports or identity cards need to be shown. There is an admission charge and dress code of jacket and tie for men.

## LONDON CLUBS

London Clubs International operates some of the city's most prestigious and exclusive casinos, from venues offering high stakes and fine dining in elegant surroundings to more popular, lively clubs. Access is restricted to members, and visitors to London should apply for membership beforehand (see page 157).

**The Palm Beach** is one of the largest and most elegant casinos in London. It attracts a young, cosmopolitan clientele who enjoy the combination of fine dining and sophisticated gaming.

LEFT *Gilded furniture, crystal chandeliers, and mirrors epitomize the elegance of a bygone era in the Salon Madame de Pompadour at Baden Baden Casino.*

RIGHT *One of the most exclusive gambling clubs in London is 50 St. James, located in an opulent regency mansion. Entrance is reserved for members only.*

**Les Ambassadeurs** is set in a building dating back nearly 200 years. Discretion and service are hallmarks of this friendly yet intimate casino offering roulette, blackjack, and punto banco.

**The Golden Nugget** has lower minimum stakes than other London casinos. Games include roulette, blackjack, punto banco, stud poker, and slot machines.

The exclusive upmarket **50 St. James**, first opened in 1828, has recently been restored to its former glory. In the gaming hall, the walls are covered with pure silk damask, and the floors are carpeted with a design from the 1820s. Two *salons privés* offer high stakes roulette, blackjack, and punto banco. Membership is compulsory, but out-of-town visitors can obtain complimentary membership between 2 p.m. and 9 p.m.. Dress is smart, and men are required to wear jackets.

# AUSTRALIA

## CROWN CASINO

The Crown Casino and Entertainment Complex on the banks of Melbourne's Yarra River opened in 1997. It includes a five-star hotel, convention facilities, riverside restaurants, boutiques, and an entertainment area.

The Atrium entrance is designed to give the effect of four seasons in a day with a subtle blend of light, water, clouds, glass, and black Italian marble combining to make a stunning display. Created by artists, composers, and technical experts, the five-story-high space features a crystal wave ceiling and laser lights.

Crown is one of the largest casinos in the southern hemisphere, offering 350 table games and 2500 slots.

## JUPITERS

Jupiters hotel, casino, and leisure complex is located on Broadbeach Island in the heart of Queensland's Gold Coast, Australia's favorite vacation destination. The buildings are set amid 15 acres (6ha) of lush, land-scaped, subtropical gardens and parkland.

The 60,100 sq ft (5574m²) casino covers two levels, and the action takes place 24 hours a day. There are 88 gaming tables and 1176 slots. Games include roulette, blackjack, baccarat, craps, Caribbean stud poker, pai gow, two-up, keno, and Jupiters Wheel. Stakes vary from A$1 to A$10,000. Admission is free, but players must be over 18 years. The exclusive Club Conrad, which caters for high rollers and serious gamblers, offers baccarat, roulette, and blackjack.

Facilities include Fortunes nightclub, with the latest video and sound effects. Nine bars, six restaurants, and an English-style pub cater to all dining tastes. Jupiter's Theater, a 1120-seat auditorium, is the venue for live performances by top acts. Recreation options include swimming, tennis, squash, and a jogging track.

LEFT *Melbourne's Crown Casino is one of the largest casinos in the southern hemisphere. The eight gaming rooms are spread across almost a third of a mile.*

# WINNERS

Roulette is one of the most popular casino games in the world, due mainly to the large odds that it pays. A winning number on roulette pays 35 to 1, which means that a small stake can potentially turn into a fortune if a player has a winning streak. By reinvesting winnings, a player with a $1 initial stake could accumulate $46,000 in just three spins of the wheel.

Looking for a system to beat the wheel is a popular pastime for many players. Inspired by the success of previous winners, they spend hours carefully noting all the numbers spun on the roulette wheel. They then devote a lot of time to analyzing the results, looking for patterns that show that particular numbers are spun with a greater frequency than others.

Casino operators do not mind players doing this, and even supply paper and pens specifically for this purpose. The operators feel secure in the knowledge that the roulette wheels are regularly balanced, so it is unlikely that a player will come up with a winning system. If a player does start winning a lot of money, casino management can easily switch the roulette wheels. If this tactic doesn't work, they have one more ace up their sleeves; they simply bar the player.

# THE MAN WHO "BROKE THE BANK" AT MONTE CARLO

The most famous roulette player of all time is the man who "broke the bank" at Monte Carlo, Charles Deville Wells, an Englishman who arrived at the casino in Monaco on July 19, 1891.

With a stake of FF100,000, he played roulette for eleven hours, winning FF250,000. He had similar good fortune on his second day at the casino. On the third day he lost FF50,000 on roulette, but recovered his loss by playing a card game called *trente et quarante,* before he returned to roulette and succeeded in breaking the bank a dozen times, winning half a million francs.

Breaking the bank in a casino does not mean that the casino is bankrupt. It simply means that the table has to replenish its float of cash chips before play can continue. At that time, as a publicity stunt in Monte Carlo, the table would be draped in a black cloth if the bank was broken. This ceremony was specially designed to attract enormous attention on the gaming floor. The black cloth would remain on the table while the float was replenished. Players would see this and be encouraged to bet more in the hope that they, too, could break the bank.

Nowadays, it is not at all unusual for the bank to be broken on a table, and it can happen several times in one night. The float is simply replenished with chips at the utmost speed, so that gaming is not interrupted.

Charles Deville Wells returned to Monte Carlo in November 1891 and continued to win. But in 1892 his luck ran out, and he began to lose heavily. He was eventually arrested in Normandy for trying to sell coal he had stolen from a steam yacht, and extradited to England. He was convicted of fraud for swindling investors in his spurious mechanical inventions and sentenced to eight years in prison. Wells' good luck on the tables was highly publicized and started a gaming boom in Monte Carlo. In 1892, a music hall song written about him became a hit in the U.K. and U.S.A.

LEFT *Monte Carlo Casino, seen here in 1913 at the height of the prewar* belle époque *period, lost a great deal of money to cheaters in the early days.*

## SPIN AND WIN

Another Englishman who had success on the roulette tables at Monte Carlo was Joseph Hobson Jaggers, a worker at a textile mill in Bradford. With his experience of the textile industry, he knew that wooden spindles were subject to wear and tear. On a visit to Monte Carlo in 1873, Jaggers was interested in the mechanics of roulette wheels. He realized that if the spindles of the roulette wheels were worn, the wheels would not be perfectly balanced. This would mean that some numbers would come up more often than others. He theorized that if he could find such a wheel, he could develop a system for winning.

Jaggers employed six clerks to record each number spun on the roulette wheels for an entire day's business. He then spent hours analyzing the data that had been collected. After six days, he discovered a wheel where nine of the numbers were spun with greater frequency than the others. He began gambling, and four days later he had won $300,000.

The casino retaliated by switching the wheels around after the close of business, and the following day Jaggers lost heavily. He then realized that a small scratch he'd noticed on the winning wheel was missing. Searching through the casino, he rediscovered his lucky wheel and resumed play, winning $450,000.

The casino then changed the design of the wheels. The fret (metal strip) that separates the numbers was made movable. Each night, the operators put the fret in a different position. Jaggers started losing and decided to quit gambling, retiring with a profit of $325,000—the equivalent of over $3 million today.

In 1880, Monte Carlo was the venue for another coup on the roulette tables. This time a team of 18 Italians operated in shifts, playing for 12 hours a day over a period of two months. Their efforts paid off with a win of $160,000, equivalent to around $1.5 million today. Big wins on roulette have also been recorded in more recent years.

TOP RIGHT *In 1947, Albert Hibbs and Roy Walford used perseverance and a simple betting system to win significant amounts at roulette in two Reno casinos.*

In 1947, Chicago graduates Albert Hibbs and Roy Walford took a motorcycle trip to Reno, Nevada. After studying the frequency of the numbers spun on the roulette wheel at the Palace Club, they determined that number nine was a particularly good bet. With a stake of $100, the pair started playing roulette. After 40 hours, they had won $5000. The Palace retaliated by switching the wheel but, confident they had a winning system, Hibbs and Walford went on to another club, Harolds. Using the same method, they increased their win to $14,500. Then they started to lose heavily and, with just $6500 left, decided it was time to quit.

Their success gained them so much publicity that when they went to the Pioneer Club in Las Vegas a year later, a casino manager recognized them. As a publicity stunt, he staked them $500 and invited them to try their luck at roulette. Hibbs and Walford put their system into action. After one month's play, they had won $33,000, but their winning streak was brought to an abrupt end when the owner asked them to leave.

In 1986, Billy Walters challenged the Golden Nugget in Atlantic City to a "freeze-out" game of roulette.

## THE WORLD'S BIGGEST SLOT MACHINE JACKPOT

Slot machines are always popular because they pay out potentially huge jackpots for small stakes. A Las Vegas woman won the world's biggest slot machine jackpot in January 2000 at the Desert Inn on The Strip. After staking just $27, she won nearly $35 million on the Nevada Megabucks slot machine. The jackpot is paid out to winners over a 25-year period, and shortly after winning she received her first installment—a check for over $1 million. The Nevada Megabucks slot machines are located in 157 Nevada casinos. Each time a machine is played at any location, the jackpot increases until it is eventually won.

## USING COMPUTERS TO WIN

Casinos ban players from using computers while on the gaming floor, as the rate at which computers process information can help players win. Spotting a pattern on roulette or keeping track of cards dealt at blackjack is made easier with a computer. New technology poses problems for casinos, because computers are getting smaller and can be easily concealed.

An interesting use of computers occurred in 1977, when a U.S. team led by Ken Uston developed a computer that could be built into shoes and programmed to help players win at blackjack. Data was fed in by using the toes to manipulate buttons, and information was relayed back by spikes which touched different parts of the feet. The shoe computers netted the team over $100,000 at an Atlantic City casino. As a result, one of the computers was confiscated and investigated by the F.B.I., who concluded that the team had not cheated, as the computer had processed public information.

The terms he proposed were that he would deposit $2 million at the cash point, which the casino was required to match. Walters said he would play until either he had won the casino's $2 million, or the casino had won his. Management agreed, and play commenced. With each spin of the wheel, Walters played bets of $2000 on five numbers. After 18 hours of play, he had won the casino's $2 million stake. He then asked if the casino wanted to continue playing. Expecting to get its money back, management agreed. Walters eventually decided to quit when he had won $3.8 million.

Plenty of other gamblers have had success at the roulette tables. In 1958, two students from Nevada, known as the Jones boys, played eight neighboring numbers on one roulette wheel for 40 hours and won $20,000. Their winning streak was cut short by the casino management, who promptly barred them.

In Argentina, two teams of players, headed by Artemeo Delgado and Helmut Berlin, won over $1 million on roulette over a period of four years.

After Dr. Richard Jarecki was barred from the casino in Monte Carlo for excessive wins, he tried his luck at San Remo in Italy. His journey paid off when he won more than $1 million from playing roulette. In 1981 it took a team of players headed by Pierre Basieux just five months to win over $150,000 in Monte Carlo.

LEFT *Progressive jackpots, which link together slot machines in a casino or an area, offer huge returns for a small investment, but do not pay out very often.*

RIGHT *Cheaters will always find a way, as depicted by these innovative cardsharps in Irving Sinclair's 1944 oil painting* The Poker Game.

# CHEATS

Cheating is as old as gambling itself. Archeological digs of Roman relics have turned up dice made from various materials including ivory, gold, silver, and gemstones, but loaded dice have also been found. Dice are loaded by incorporating weights on one side to make them land more frequently on desired numbers.

There are many ways to cheat at card games. In poker, knowing your opponents' hands is extremely useful. This is achieved by marking the backs of certain cards in a subtle way so they can be "read" by the cheat. Methods used include applying a small amount of a chemical that shines or glows, or using a spiked implement to make an indentation in the card.

A skilled cardsharp can shuffle the cards in an apparently normal manner, but will put them into a specific order to ensure he gets a good hand. Cutting the cards is not a problem. A card with a slight crease down the center is used to mark the cut, and a quick one-handed shuffle puts the cards back into their original position. A cardsharp can also deal cards from the bottom of the pack, or deal the second card from the top, saving the top card for himself.

Values are printed on the corner of cards, so cheats need to see just a small piece to know another player's hand. Metallic lighters, glass ashtrays, and specially adapted rings containing mirrors are used as reflectors. The cheat positions the object on the table, and passes them over the reflector as the cards are dealt.

Cheats also collude with one another. Working in a team, they make prearranged signals to ensure that the player with the best hand stays in the game, while all others fold.

Cheating seldom pays, especially not for some 19th-century professional gamblers who made their living on the Mississippi riverboats. Their profits came more from cheating than from fair play, resulting in the lynching of five cardsharps in 1835.

Gaming is all about winning and losing, so it makes sense to manage your money effectively. It is very easy to get carried away by the excitement and lose your stake. By understanding the rules of the game, the odds paid, the chances of winning, and when to quit, players can ensure their casino experience is pleasant.

Gambling should be treated like any other form of entertainment. Expect to spend your money and have a good time doing so. Unfortunately, most gamblers not only want to win, they actually expect to win and can take it extremely badly when they lose. Once the initial stake has been lost, they attempt to get it back by making increased bets. Most gamblers do not keep records of how much they win or lose. Big wins are fondly remembered, while losses tend to be forgotten. Even professional gamblers can delude themselves into thinking they either always win or break even.

## STAYING SOLVENT

• Take care of your chips and money, and beware of criminals who use the the distraction of the games to pick pockets and snatch chips.

• Only exchange chips or money with casino staff. There may be a line at the cash point, but at least you will be sure you are not being passed counterfeit money or chips. Ask for big wins to be paid by check.

• Only bet money you can afford to lose. If you gamble regularly, set a budget for gambling and stick to it. Limit the amount of cash you take to the casino and leave check books, cash cards, and credit cards at home if you think you will be tempted to use them.

• Many casinos have cash machines (A.T.M.s) on the gaming floor, making it easy to obtain money. Avoid credit facilities. If you haven't got it, don't spend it!

• Learn how to play the games by reading the rules provided by most casinos. Most players do not learn the rules until something goes wrong.

• Rules of play may differ in various countries so be sure you understand the rules where you are playing.

If you need anything explained, speak to a casino manager—do not rely on the advice of other players.

• Understand the odds and compare the true odds of each game to the odds paid by the casino. Some games offer better value than others. Each game has a variety of bets, often with different house advantages (see page 152). On some bets, this is so high that the bet is not worth playing. Find out the house advantages for individual bets before you begin playing.

• Although many games rely on luck, in blackjack and poker, the outcome can be influenced by skill. If you play card games, practice them at home. Novice poker players are a great source of income for professionals, as an inexperienced player is no match for someone with years of experience.

• Many casinos offer regular lessons to explain the games, and it is worth attending these. Watch other players in action. It costs nothing to be a spectator, and a lot can be learned from experienced players.

• Don't forget that winning bets on roulette are left to ride. Many players leave the table and forget they still have a bet on the next spin. It is usually left to ride for three spins. A bet straight up on a number is capable of winning 105 chips before it is removed. If you do not claim your winnings you will lose them.

• Take account of the additional costs involved in visiting a casino. Transport, tips, admission charges or membership fees, refreshments, and other nongaming activities—such as shows, cinemas, shopping, and sports facilities—can add up if costs are not monitored.

## SUBLIMINAL PRACTICES

Casinos use a variety of subliminal practices to ensure they get the maximum amount of money from visitors before they get anywhere near a gaming table.

Casino design is no accident. Almost every feature is built in with profit in mind. Exteriors are lavish, and use every marketing trick in the book to get players to walk through the door. This is taken to the extreme in

Las Vegas, where shows put on outside the casinos get people to stop and watch, and, hopefully, go inside.

Many resort casinos have adjacent shopping malls. One moment you're browsing around a shop, the next you're inside a casino. Some casinos in Las Vegas are connected to neighboring casinos by monorails and moving sidewalks.

Casino operators know that the longer a player remains inside the gaming hall, the more money he or she will spend, so every need is catered for. If you are a hotel guest, a valet will park your car, while day visitors are provided with transport from the parking lot to the casino entrance.

Waiters deliver food and drinks directly to the gaming tables. Many casinos supply free alcohol, as they know that a drunken player is less likely to care about losing. As many casinos are situated in hotels, players can simply sleep off their hangover on the premises.

Casinos have gone to great lengths to ensure that players do not get bored, by offering every type of high quality entertainment, from lavish variety shows to live sports events and a full range of sports facilities.

Players' awareness of time is reduced. Casinos do not have clocks, and the dealers do not wear watches. In the artificial environment, it is always nighttime.

On entering the gaming hall, players encounter the slot machines. The flashing lights, bright colors, high noise levels, and the hope of winning a big jackpot are all designed to attract customers. The slot machines are deliberately positioned so that players spend all their loose change on their way into and out of the casino. The slots are the most profitable games for the casino as they pay out on average only 75 to 80 percent of the total amount staked.

A recent innovation has been the development of an odor that makes players bet more on the slot machines. It was developed by the US-based Smell and Taste Treatment and Research Foundation. In trials carried out in Las Vegas, slots adapted to emit the odor produced a 45 percent increase in business.

Visitors who just take a look inside a casino out of curiosity might be handed a few gaming chips. As these can only be exchanged at the tables, they are encouraged to place a few bets.

Players' associations with "real" money can decrease when they exchange their cash for a pile of seemingly worthless plastic chips. An entire stack fits nicely into your hand, and its tempting to put a number of chips on a single bet. Cash chips have a value printed on them, but table chips do not, so it is very easy to forget their worth. Smart cards and coinless gaming reduce the link with cash even further.

At first glance, the advertised minimum stake for a casino may seem low. However, casinos normally only have a few low-staking tables or slot machines which are usually very crowded, especially over weekends or vacation periods. To get into a more relaxed game, it is necessary to up your stakes.

If a player appears to be on a winning streak, a technique called "stepping up" is employed by the dealer, who will make up payouts with chips of a slightly higher denomination. If the player continues to win, the value of the chips will be increased again. This is to subtly tempt the player to bet with the higher value chips. By betting higher stakes, players will lose their winnings more quickly.

Casinos hire attractive, friendly personnel. Players wandering around the gaming hall may pass an empty roulette table. The dealer will smile in welcome and spin the wheel. Out of curiosity, most players stop and watch to see where the ball will land. With a captive audience, the dealer will quickly spin again. The spectators will soon be tempted to play.

Table games are played at a fast pace, which gives players little time to think. There is hardly any time between games to count your chips. On roulette, for example, there is an average of one spin a minute. Experienced players know that you don't have to bet each time, but novices often rush to place new bets, particularly if they have won on the last round.

## GAMES OF CHANCE AND SKILL

Casinos offer a choice between games of skill, where the player can affect the outcome, and games of chance, where players have no input and rely on luck.

Games of chance include roulette, slots, and baccarat. Once players have decided what numbers to play, there is no further action to take.

Poker and blackjack are games of skill. As players make all the decisions about taking cards, they are able to use their intelligence to win. With games of skill, a combination of knowledge and experience can make the difference between winning and losing.

## UNDERSTANDING THE ODDS

The odds tell players how much they could win for a particular stake. Odds are quoted for each type of bet in a game. Some odds are printed directly on the betting layout (for example, "Insurance pays 2 to 1" on blackjack tables), but these are only some of the many bets that can be played, each offering different odds.

A sign listing all the odds for a particular game will be on the table, hanging over it, or close by. The list gives the name of the bet and the odds paid, allowing players to decide how they want to bet.

The odds are quoted as two numbers, like 2 to 1, or 8 to 1. The number on the left is the amount won if the number on the right is staked. For odds of 2 to 1, if one chip is staked two chips will be won and the player keeps the stake, so a total of three chips will be won. For odds of 3 to 2, if 1 chip is staked, one and a half chips will be won and the player keeps the stake. Total winnings are therefore two and a half chips. For a five-chip bet on odds of 2 to 1, five multiplies the odds so 2 to 1 becomes 10 to 5. This means that for a five-chip bet, 10 chips are won and the player keeps the stake, giving total winnings of 15 chips.

An alternative way of writing the odds is to put a slash or a colon between the two numbers, so 2 to 1 becomes 2/1 or 2:1.

## EVENS

The odds of evens are an exception, as no numbers are quoted. It is actually odds of one to one (1/1) and is often called "even money." The outside bets on roulette (black, red; even, odd; high, low) are often called the even chances, because they pay odds of evens. A $10 bet on an even chance pays $20. ($10 is the winnings and $10 is the returned stake.)

## UNDERSTANDING PROBABILITY

If a coin is tossed, there is a 50 percent chance that it will land on heads, and a 50 percent chance that it will land on tails. However, this does not mean that if you toss a coin 100 times, it will actually land 50 times on heads and 50 times on tails. After a large number of tosses, the number of heads and tails will be approximately equal, but there is no way that the outcome of one particular toss can be predicted.

When betting on roulette, many players make the mistake of assuming that because a number has not been spun for a long time, it must be due. Over time it will be spun again, but a player could wait all night for a specific number to come up.

## HOUSE ADVANTAGE

The odds paid by casinos for winning bets on most games are not the true chances of winning the game. Casinos make a profit by paying out bets at odds that are less than the true chances of winning. This difference is called the "house advantage" or "edge," and it is usually stated as a percentage.

The house advantage for different games varies (see table opposite). For some games, such as blackjack, an average is quoted, as the house advantage changes throughout the game.

Using roulette as an example, you can see how the house advantage works. A roulette wheel with one zero is marked with the numbers 1–36 inclusive, plus zero. This gives a possible 37 numbers that can be spun. By placing a bet on every single number, players can guarantee that they will have a win. This would cost the player 37 chips. The player will be paid odds of 35 to 1 for the winning number. That means he or she would win 36 (35 + 1) chips. However, since it cost 37 chips, the player has actually lost one chip. If a player continues in this manner, eventually all his or her chips will end up with the casino, as every spin of the wheel would cost one chip.

Casinos come off even better on a roulette wheel with two zeros. Now there are 38 numbers—but the odds paid for a winning number remain the same at 35 to 1. If one chip is bet on every number, the casino wins two chips on every spin of the wheel. By adding an extra zero, the casino has doubled its profits.

COMPARISON OF HOUSE ADVANTAGE
ON DIFFERENT GAMES

|  | % |
| --- | --- |
| Blackjack | 5.6 |
| Dice | from >1 – 16.7* |
| Punto Banco | up to 5 |
| Roulette with one zero | 2.7 |
| Roulette with two zeros | 5.26 |
| (* depends on the type of bet). | |

## COMMISSION

On games such as dice and baccarat, the casino pays true odds on some bets, but charges a commission on the payout. This is usually a percentage of the stake, but is sometimes a percentage of the winnings.

In poker, where players bet among themselves, the casino charges either a percentage of the pot or an hourly rate. Poker is open to many ways of cheating, but by using casino facilities, players can ensure they are playing fair games.

## SETTING A STAKE LEVEL

Your gaming budget will determine your stake level. If you start with $1000, for example, betting one chip per spin on a $10 roulette table will last 100 spins. With a spin a minute, you will be able to gamble for at least an hour and 40 minutes. If you bet 10 chips per spin, you could lose your money in 10 minutes.

The ideal is to determine in advance how much you intend to spend and how long you would like to play, and then place bets at a stake level and frequency that will allow you to enjoy your gaming.

On roulette, although it is tempting to bet on every spin, players are not obliged to do so, and you will have more time to think if you bet less frequently.

On blackjack, you may also bet on another player's hand. While learning the game this is a good tactic, as it offers a useful way of gaining experience if you are not yet confident in your ability to play.

## CHECKING PAYOUTS

Learn how to calculate the winnings on your bets. Due to the speed at which the games are dealt, casinos can make mistakes. Winning bets are sometimes missed, and payouts can be incorrectly calculated.

Confusion can arise when chips are worth more than one stake unit. The inspector checks only large payouts. If you disagree with a payout, query it with the inspector. If necessary, the camera can be checked to verify your claim.

## KEEPING RECORDS

Keep a notebook to record your gambling and to help you judge how well you are playing. It is very easy to delude yourself into thinking that you do not lose. If your records reveal that you are losing too much, then you can analyze what is going wrong and take measures to reduce your losses. Maybe you need more practice, or you need to modify your betting strategy.

# PROBLEM GAMING

In the United States you will find the record useful if you have a big win, as gambling wins are subject to tax. Players can offset gambling losses against winnings, but the IRS requires players to keep an accurate record of dates, bets made, address of gaming establishment, names of people with you, and the amount won or lost. Comps also count as winnings. In addition, proof of expenditure, like casino receipts and bank records, will need to be shown if you are audited.

## TIPPING

Policies vary depending on local legislation. British law prohibits the tipping of gaming staff, but nongaming staff (such as waiters or car valets) may receive tips. In the United States it is normal to tip just about everyone. The amount you give is entirely discretionary. At the gaming tables it is usual to give the dealer a tip when you cash in your chips. In Europe, where tips make up a large part of their earnings, the dealers are quite blunt and will remind players not to forget them.

## DECIDING WHEN TO QUIT

"Quit when you're ahead" is an old saying that makes sense in gaming. As soon as a winning streak stops, take your chips to the cash point and leave. It is easy to fall into the trap of having one last bet, until you run out of chips and your big win has disappeared.

One strategy is to just bet with your original stake money and go home when it is used up. Any winnings are cashed in and saved for the next time.

## PROBLEM GAMBLING

Most people are able to enjoy gambling without it becoming a problem in their lives, but for a small number of people it can become addictive. No matter how hard they try, they may not be able to break the cycle and regain control of their gambling.

The first step toward solving addictive or compulsive gambling is to recognize that there is a problem. Some signs are:
- you view gambling as a way of earning money
- you gamble with money that is intended for living expenses such as rent, food, or transport
- you continually exceed your budget
- you need to borrow because you have gambled too much, and then end up gambling even more to try and pay back the loans
- all your free time is spent gambling
- you neglect family, friends, and work in order to concentrate on gambling.

There are many international and local support organizations, such as Gamblers Anonymous, who are there to offer help. If you feel your gambling is getting out of hand, contact one of them before it is too late. Most have toll-free lines that enable you to speak to a trained councillor over the phone. Many hold regular meetings where compulsive gamblers can discuss their problems and find solutions. There are also organizations that support the families of gamblers.

Most casinos support responsible gambling, as they understand the importance of promoting gaming as an integral part of the worldwide entertainment and leisure industry. Many have established their own counselling services and assist state or national responsible gaming programs and support organizations with funding, and by handing out brochures or putting up posters advertising their services. Your family doctor may also be able to offer advice on counselling services in your area.

Problem gaming can affect anyone, regardless of age, race, gender, or social status. As with other forms of addiction, there is no way of telling in advance who might develop problems with gambling, but early intervention, followed by treatment, care, and support are the first steps to recovery.

Gaming should be fun—just remember to gamble with your head and not with your heart.

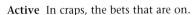 

**Active** In craps, the bets that are on.

**All-in** A poker player who runs out of funds, but still plays for the portion of the pot he has contributed to.

**Anchor box** Where the player sits who is dealt the first cards in blackjack (also called first base).

**Basic strategy** A method of play used to reduce the house advantage in blackjack.

**Biscuit** A high denomination cash chip.

**Bluff** To pretend you have a good hand (in poker).

**Burned cards** In blackjack, cards discarded from the deck without being seen by other players.

**Bust** A score over 21 in blackjack (a losing hand).

**Cage** The cash point on the gaming floor.

**Call** To bet the same as the previous bet.

**Cold deck** Deck of cards arranged in a specific order.

**Color** Table chips on roulette.

**Comp** Complimentary benefits for favored players.

**Court cards** King, Queen, Jack (see also Picture cards).

**Croupier** The dealer.

**Cut card** A blank card used for cutting a deck of cards to denote where it must be reshuffled.

**Dolly** Marker showing the winning roulette number.

**Draw** To take another card (also called to hit).

**Drop box** A hidden box on the gaming table where the dealer puts money received for bets or chips.

**Edge** The profit a casino makes on bets. It is usually expressed as a percentage (see also House Advantage).

**Fold** To surrender from a game of poker.

**Forced bet** The bet required to be made by one poker player to get the betting started.

**High roller** A high staking player.

**Hole card** The dealer's down card in blackjack; cards in the players' hands in poker.

**House advantage** The profit a casino makes on bets, usually expressed as a percentage (see also Edge).

**Load** To add weights to dice so they always land on a particular side.

**Marker** An amount of money granted on credit to a player, that he or she owes to the casino (an I.O.U.).

**Money laundering** Processing illegally acquired funds through a legitimate business. Criminals engaged in this activity have favored the casino industry in the past, because of the ease with which large amounts of cash flows into and out of a casino.

**Monkey** A British term for a £500 bet.

**Muck pile** Where the losing cards are placed in poker.

**Natural** A score of 8 or 9 in baccarat; a score of 21 dealt as the original hand in blackjack.

**Odds** The chances of winning.

**Open** To make the first bet.

**Pass** To take no further cards.

**Picture cards** King, Queen, Jack (see also Court cards).

**Pit** A group of gaming tables.

**Plaque** A high denomination cash chip.

**Pony** A British term for a £25 bet.

**Ponte/Punto** The player in baccarat or punto banco.

**Pot** The total stakes that are played for in poker.

**Progressive slots** Slots where the jackpot increases each time a new coin is inserted for play. A number of slot machines may be linked into one large jackpot.

**Punter** A gambler.

**Raise** To make an increased bet.

**Riffle shuffle** When the card pack is split into two and shuffled by letting the cards drop, using both thumbs so that they concertina together. The cards are then pushed together to form one pile.

**Sabot** A box where cards are placed for dealing.

**Salon privé** Private room reserved for high rollers.

**Seed the pot** When each player in poker makes a bet of equal value to start the game.

**Shoe** Box where cards are placed for dealing.

**Shooter** The person who throws the dice in craps.

**Showdown** When poker players reveal their hands.

**Single** Minimum denomination chip (£1, $1 etc.).

**Stake** The amount of money bet.

**Stand** To take no more cards.

**Standoff** A tie in blackjack.

**Toke** A tip (usually given to the dealer).

**Valet** Person employed to park customer's cars.

**Vigorish** Commission paid in craps.

All telephone numbers are given with national codes. Consult your directory or operator for international dialling codes. Numbers listed as toll free apply only when dialled from inside the relevant country.

**U.S.A. AND CARIBBEAN**

THE VENETIAN

3355 Las Vegas Boulevard South, Las Vegas 89101

Tel:      (702) 414-1000

Fax:      (702) 414-4884

Web:      www.venetian.com

Reservations: 1-888-283-6423.

PARIS LAS VEGAS

3655 Las Vegas Boulevard South, Las Vegas 89101

Tel:      (702) 967-4401

Fax:      (702) 967-4925

Reservations: 1-888-266-5687.

LUXOR

3900 Las Vegas Boulevard South, Las Vegas 89101

Tel:      (702) 262-4822

Fax:      (702) 262-4825

Web:      www.luxor.com

Reservations: 1-800-288-1000.

MGM GRAND

3799 Las Vegas Boulevard South, Las Vegas 89101

Tel:      (702) 891-111 or (702) 891-777

Web:      www.mgmgrand.com

Reservations: 1-800-929-1111.

MGM MIRAGE / BELLAGIO / TREASURE ISLAND

3799 Las Vegas Boulevard South, Las Vegas 89101

Tel:      (702) 891-3430

Fax:      (702) 891-7270

Web:      www.mirageresorts.com

Bellagio:

3600 Las Vegas Boulevard, Las Vegas 89101

Treasure Island:

3300 Las Vegas Boulevard, Las Vegas 89101.

CIRCUS CIRCUS

2880 Las Vegas Boulevard, Las Vegas 89101

Tel:      (702) 734-0410

Web:      www.circuscircus-lasvegas.com

Reservations: 1-800-444-circus.

EXCALIBUR

3850 Las Vegas Boulevard South, Las Vegas 89101

Web:      www.excalibur-casino.com

Reservations: 1-800-811-4320.

NEW YORK NEW YORK

3790 Las Vegas Boulevard South, Las Vegas 89101

Tel:      (702) 740-6969

Fax:      (702) 740-6700.

LAS VEGAS HILTON

3000 Paradise Road, Las Vegas 89101

Reservations: 1-800-732-7171.

BINION'S HORSESHOE

128 East Fremont Street, Las Vegas 89101

Reservations: 1-800-622-6468.

BALLY'S

3645 Las Vegas Boulevard South, Las Vegas 89101

Reservations: 1-800-634-3434.

CAESARS PALACE

3570 Las Vegas Boulevard South, Las Vegas 89101

Reservations: 1-800-634-6661.

LAS VEGAS TOURISM: www.lasvegastourism.com

MOHEGAN SUN

1 Mohegan Sun Blvd, Uncasville, Connecticut 06382

Tel:      (860) 204-7100

Fax:      (860) 204-7155

Email:    hotelsales@mtga.com

Web:      www.mohegan.nsn.us

Reservations: 1-877-204-7100.

BEAU RIVAGE

875 Beach Boulevard, Biloxi, Mississippi 39530

Tel:    (228) 386-7111

Fax:    (228)386-7471

Email:    reservations@beaurivageresort.com

Web:    www.beaurivage.com

Reservations: 1-888-567-6667.

ATLANTIS

Paradise Island, New Providence Island, Bahamas

PO Box N-4777, Nassau, Bahamas

Tel:    (242) 363-3000

Fax:    (242) 363-3524

Web:    www.AtlantisResort.com

**EUROPE**

MONTE CARLO

Place du Casino, Monte Carlo, Monaco

Tel:    92 16 20 00

Fax:    92 16 38 62

web:    www.casino-monte-carlo.com

BADEN BADEN

1 Kaiserallee, Baden Baden 76530, Germany

Tel:    (7221) 21060

Fax:    (7221) 21654

email:    info@Casino-baden-baden.de

web:    www.casino-baden-baden.de

LONDON CLUBS INTERNATIONAL

Visitors should direct membership enquiries to:-

10 Brick Street, London W1J 7HQ

Freephone: 07000 707 606

Web:    www.clublci.com

**AUSTRALIA AND NEW ZEALAND**

CONRAD JUPITERS

Broadbeach Island, Queensland 4218, Australia

Tel:    (7) 5592-1133

Fax:    (7) 5592-8219

Web:    www.goldcoast.conradinternational.com

CROWN CASINO

8 Whiteman Street, Southbank, Melbourne, Victoria 3006, Australia

Tel:    (3) 9292-8888

Fax:    (3) 9292-6600

Web:    www.crownltd.com.au

Reservations: 1-800-811653.

SKY CITY

Federal House, 86 Federal St, Auckland, New Zealand

Tel:    (9) 363-6000

Fax:    (9) 363-6010

Email:    reservations@skycity.co.nz

Web:    www.skycity.co.nz

Reservations: 0800 759-2489.

**SOUTH AFRICA**

SUN CITY & THE PALACE OF THE LOST CITY

Northwest Province, South Africa

PO Box 2, Sun City 0316, South Africa

Tel:    (14) 557-1000

Fax:    (14) 557-3895

Web:    www.sunint.com

Reservations: (11) 780-7800.

GRANDWEST CASINO & ENTERTAINMENT CENTRE

1 Vanguard Drive, Cape Town, South Africa

Tel:    (21) 505-7777

Web:    www.grandwest.co.za

**GAMBLERS ANONYMOUS**

International Service Office:

PO Box 17173, Los Angeles, CA 90017

Tel:    (213) 386-8789

Fax:    (213) 386-0030

Web:    www.gamblersanonymous.org

Email:    isomain@gamblersanonymous.org

This is an international fellowship of men and women who share their experience, strength and hope to help others recover from gambling problems. Regular meetings are held in cities worldwide.

# Credits & Acknowledgments

All cover photography by Ryno Reyneke, except spine (Photo Access/G Buss). All other photography by Ryno Reyneke with the exception of those supplied by photographers and/or agencies as listed below. Key to Locations: tr = top right; bl = bottom left; br = bottom right; l = left.

BAL = Bridgeman Art Library

BAL[1]: *Playing with Dice*. From Lo Libro de Multi Belli Miracuti et de li Vicii (14th century). British Library.

BAL[2]: *A Kick Up at a Hazard Table*. Thomas Rowlandson (1756–1827). Private Collection.

BAL[3]: *The Casino Monte Carlo*. Christian Ludwig Bokelman (1844–94). Christie's Image's.

BAL[4]: *The Cheat with the Ace of Clubs*. Georges de la Tour (1593–1652). Preston Hall Museum, Stockton-on-Tees.

BAL[5]: *The Poker Game*. Irving Sinclair (1895–1969). Private Collection.

BAL[6]: *The Dice Players*. Georges de la Tour (1593–1652). Preston Hall Museum, Stockton-on-Tees.

BAL[7]: *A Showdown*. Albert Beck Wenzell (1864–1917). Museum of the City of New York.

BAL[8]: *The Roulette Table at Monte Carlo*. Edvard Munch (1863–1944). Munch-Museet, Oslo, Norway.

CI = Corbis Images

GM = Gauselmann Museum

GI/HG = Gallo Images/Hulton Getty.

GI/TS = Gallo Images/ Tony Stone (BS = Brian Stablyk; SC = Stewart Cohen; DN = Donald Nausbaum; GA = Gregg Adams; SP = Steven Peters).

GS = Great Stock (BB = Bill Brooks; BR = Bryan Reinhart; JP = José Pelaez; LL = Lester Lefkowitz; MK = Michael Keller; RM = Rob Matheson; WT = Wes Thompson).

I = Inpra (JD = J Donoso; RD = Ros Drinkwater; SC = Stephane Compoint).

LV = Las Vegas News Bureau Collection, University of Nevada, Las Vegas Library.

N/AR = Nimatallah/Art Resource.

W = Worshipful Company of Makers of Playing Cards. Guildhall Library, London.

A = Atlantis, Bahamas; AF = Athol Franz; B = Bellagio, Las Vegas; BB = Baden Baden, Germany; CC = Crown Casino, Melbourne; FR = Frank Reynolds; GL = Geisha Lounge; HL = Holger Leue; M = Mirage, Las Vegas; MC = Monte Carlo, Las Vegas; MGM = MGM Grand, Las Vegas; MS = Mohegan Sun, Connecticut; RS = Robin Smith; SC = Sky City, Auckland; SJ = St. James, London; TS = Treasure Island, Las Vegas; V = The Venetian, Las Vegas.

| | | | | | | | | | | |
|---|---|---|---|---|---|---|---|---|---|---|
| 1 | | I/JD | 22 | LV | 95 | | GI/HG | 131 | | I/SC |
| 2 | | I/SC | 23 | LV | 101 | | BAL[6] | 133 | | MS |
| 5 | | HL | 24 | GS/MK | 115 | | GI/HG | 134 | | A |
| 6 | | FR | 25 | GL | 118 | | V | 135 | | A |
| 7 | | GI/TS/GA | 27 | HL | 119 | | TS | 137 | | GS/BR |
| 9 | | GI/TS/SP | 28 | B | 120 | | GS/LL | 138 | | BB |
| 10 | | GI/TS/BS | 31 | CC | 122 | | GS/BB | 139 | | SJ |
| 12 | | BAL[1] | 35 | CC | 123 | | B | 140 | | CC |
| 13 | | N/AR | 50 | MC | 124 | bl | FR | 141 | l | SC |
| 14 | | BAL[2] | 53 | BAL[4] | | br | RS | | br | SC |
| 15 | | GI/HG | 54 | SC | 125 | bl | FR | 143 | | AF |
| 16 | | W | 66 | MC | | br | HL | 144 | | GI/TS/DN |
| 17 | | W | 68 | I/RD | 126 | | MGM | 145 | | BAL[7] |
| 18 | | GI/HG | 79 | BAL[5] | 127 | | GS/RM | 146 | | G/H |
| 19 | tr | GM | 84 | GI/HG | 128 | | M | 147 | | CI |
| | bl | GM | 85 | SC | 129 | | GS/WT | 148 | | GI/TS/SC |
| 21 | | BAL[3] | 88 | GS/JP | 130 | | V | 149 | | BAL[8] |

The publishers would like to thank the following for assisting with photo shoots: Sun City, South Africa: Frank Devenney, casino manager; Bruce Ashburner, casino shift manager; Beryl Scott, senior PR manager; Colleen van Eyk, gaming marketing manager; Theresa Newman, PRO; and Alistair Macgregor, dealer. GrandWest Casino and Entertainment Center, Cape Town: Robin Kennedy, pit boss; Duane Firmani, security; Mark Dovale, tables manager; Dirk Geere, slots manager; Karen Rothschild, marketing manager. Peter Collins of the National Center for the Study of Gambling, Cape Town; Kevin Kevany, Kerry Capstick-Dale, Julian Richfield, Enid Vickers and Wendy Masters of Corporate Image, Cape Town; and Adrienne Courcol of Sun International South Africa.